About Math Connection:

Welcome to RBP Books' Connection series. Math Connection provides students with focused practice to help reinforce and develop math skills in all areas defined by the NCTM (National Council of Teachers of Mathematics) as appropriate for third-grade students. These include numeration and operations, three- and four-digit addition and subtraction, probability, measurement, shapes, graphing, fractions, time, money values, word problems, multiplication, and division. Exercises are grade-level appropriate with clear examples and instructions on each page to guide the lesson; they also feature a variety of activities to help students develop their ability to work with numbers.

ISBN: 1-887923-79-9

Math Connection—Grade 3
Table of Contents

...continued

Diagnostic Test 1

Solve the problems.

1.

6	7	9	8	5	9
+ 3	+ 5	+ 4	+ 7	+ 8	+ 6

2.

12	14	15	10	11	13
− 8	− 7	− 9	− 6	− 5	− 6

3.

3	4	5	2	4	8
8	6	5	3	7	3
+ 2	+ 7	+ 6	+ 5	+ 3	+ 5

Write the missing numbers.

4. 0 ___ 2 3 ___ 5 ___ ___ 8 ___ 10 ___ 12 ___ 14 15 ___ ___ 18 ___ 20

5. 34 ___ 36   47 ___ 49   59 ___ 61   72 ___ 74   83 ___ 85

Use >, <, or = to compare the numbers.

6. 34 ___ 35   23 ___ 32   39 ___ 40   27 ___ 27   29 ___ 19   78 ___ 87

Write the numbers.

7. eight _____   twelve _____   twenty _____

thirty-five _____   forty-one _____   fifty-nine _____

Math Connection—Grade 3—RBP3799   www.summerbridgeactivities.com   © RBP Books

Diagnostic Test 2

Solve the problems.

1.
| 21 | 42 | 17 | 27 | 62 | 47 |
| + 34 | + 51 | + 41 | + 52 | + 35 | + 22 |

2.
| 24 | 35 | 42 | 79 | 94 | 87 |
| − 12 | − 23 | − 31 | − 53 | − 62 | − 24 |

3.
| 37 | 73 | 29 | 41 | 27 | 84 |
| + 44 | + 28 | + 32 | + 39 | + 35 | + 76 |

4.
| 43 | 52 | 61 | 74 | 32 | 71 |
| − 28 | − 39 | − 27 | − 18 | − 19 | − 32 |

Write the time shown on these clocks.

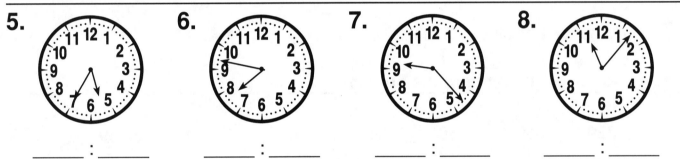

5. _____ : _____   **6.** _____ : _____   **7.** _____ : _____   **8.** _____ : _____

Draw hands to show the time on each clock.

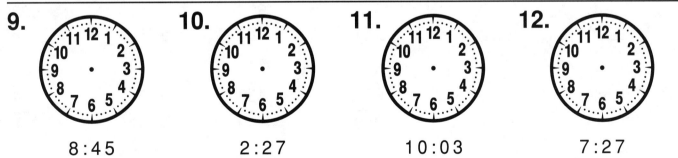

9. 8 : 45   **10.** 2 : 27   **11.** 10 : 03   **12.** 7 : 27

Count the money. Write the total.

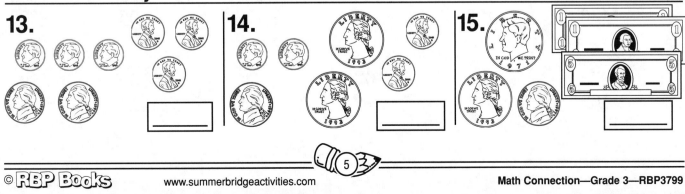

13. _____   **14.** _____   **15.** _____

Diagnostic Test 3

Solve the problems.

1. 569 equals _____ hundreds _____ tens _____ ones

2. 297 equals _____ hundreds _____ tens _____ ones

3. 4,203 equals _____ thousands _____ hundreds _____ tens _____ ones

4. What is the value of 7 in 752? _____

5. What is the value of 8 in 183? _____

6. What is the value of 9 in 1,923? _____

7. What is the value of 3 in 3,294? _____

Use >, <, or = to compare the numbers.

8. 329 ___ 239   480 ___ 408   3,490 ___ 3,409   2,189 ___ 1,892

9.
347	872	632	534	731	523
+ 232	+ 127	+ 144	+ 125	+ 241	+ 362

10.
549	238	921	458	763	344
+ 277	+ 463	+ 379	+ 226	+ 159	+ 429

11.
347	568	799	389	326	630
− 126	− 126	− 289	− 166	− 105	− 320

12.
278	480	871	732	530	703
− 169	− 348	− 646	− 356	− 218	− 543

Math Connection—Grade 3—RBP3799   www.summerbridgeactivities.com   © RBP Books

Diagnostic Test 4
Solve the problems.

1.
$$\begin{array}{r} 3 \\ \times\,5 \\ \hline \end{array}\qquad \begin{array}{r} 4 \\ \times\,2 \\ \hline \end{array}\qquad \begin{array}{r} 6 \\ \times\,4 \\ \hline \end{array}\qquad \begin{array}{r} 5 \\ \times\,7 \\ \hline \end{array}\qquad \begin{array}{r} 8 \\ \times\,7 \\ \hline \end{array}\qquad \begin{array}{r} 9 \\ \times\,3 \\ \hline \end{array}$$

2.
$$\begin{array}{r} 7 \\ \times\,6 \\ \hline \end{array}\qquad \begin{array}{r} 0 \\ \times\,8 \\ \hline \end{array}\qquad \begin{array}{r} 9 \\ \times\,9 \\ \hline \end{array}\qquad \begin{array}{r} 1 \\ \times\,7 \\ \hline \end{array}\qquad \begin{array}{r} 6 \\ \times\,5 \\ \hline \end{array}\qquad \begin{array}{r} 4 \\ \times\,8 \\ \hline \end{array}$$

3. $18 \div 3 = \underline{}$ $21 \div 7 = \underline{}$ $54 \div 9 = \underline{}$ $64 \div 8 = \underline{}$ $36 \div 6 = \underline{}$ $16 \div 4 = \underline{}$

4. $3\overline{)24}$ $2\overline{)18}$ $9\overline{)72}$ $5\overline{)25}$ $4\overline{)28}$ $8\overline{)32}$

5.
$$\begin{array}{r} 7 \\ \times\,10 \\ \hline \end{array}\qquad \begin{array}{r} 18 \\ \times\,10 \\ \hline \end{array}\qquad \begin{array}{r} 34 \\ \times\,10 \\ \hline \end{array}\qquad \begin{array}{r} 23 \\ \times\,10 \\ \hline \end{array}\qquad \begin{array}{r} 78 \\ \times\,10 \\ \hline \end{array}\qquad \begin{array}{r} 99 \\ \times\,10 \\ \hline \end{array}$$

6.
$$\begin{array}{r} 13 \\ \times\,2 \\ \hline \end{array}\qquad \begin{array}{r} 14 \\ \times\,2 \\ \hline \end{array}\qquad \begin{array}{r} 12 \\ \times\,3 \\ \hline \end{array}\qquad \begin{array}{r} 11 \\ \times\,7 \\ \hline \end{array}\qquad \begin{array}{r} 11 \\ \times\,9 \\ \hline \end{array}\qquad \begin{array}{r} 31 \\ \times\,2 \\ \hline \end{array}$$

7.
$$\begin{array}{r} 15 \\ \times\,5 \\ \hline \end{array}\qquad \begin{array}{r} 34 \\ \times\,7 \\ \hline \end{array}\qquad \begin{array}{r} 34 \\ \times\,8 \\ \hline \end{array}\qquad \begin{array}{r} 65 \\ \times\,4 \\ \hline \end{array}\qquad \begin{array}{r} 82 \\ \times\,8 \\ \hline \end{array}\qquad \begin{array}{r} 37 \\ \times\,6 \\ \hline \end{array}$$

8. $6\overline{)32}$ $5\overline{)48}$ $9\overline{)29}$ $9\overline{)78}$ $8\overline{)61}$ $6\overline{)43}$

9. $5\overline{)92}$ $5\overline{)83}$ $4\overline{)73}$ $7\overline{)82}$ $5\overline{)67}$ $6\overline{)84}$

Write the equations for each number family.

10. (4 / 6 24)

_____ x _____ = _____
_____ x _____ = _____
_____ ÷ _____ = _____
_____ ÷ _____ = _____

11. (7 / 8 56)

_____ x _____ = _____
_____ x _____ = _____
_____ ÷ _____ = _____
_____ ÷ _____ = _____

12. (9 / 4 36)

_____ x _____ = _____
_____ x _____ = _____
_____ ÷ _____ = _____
_____ ÷ _____ = _____

Diagnostic Test 5

Solve the problems.

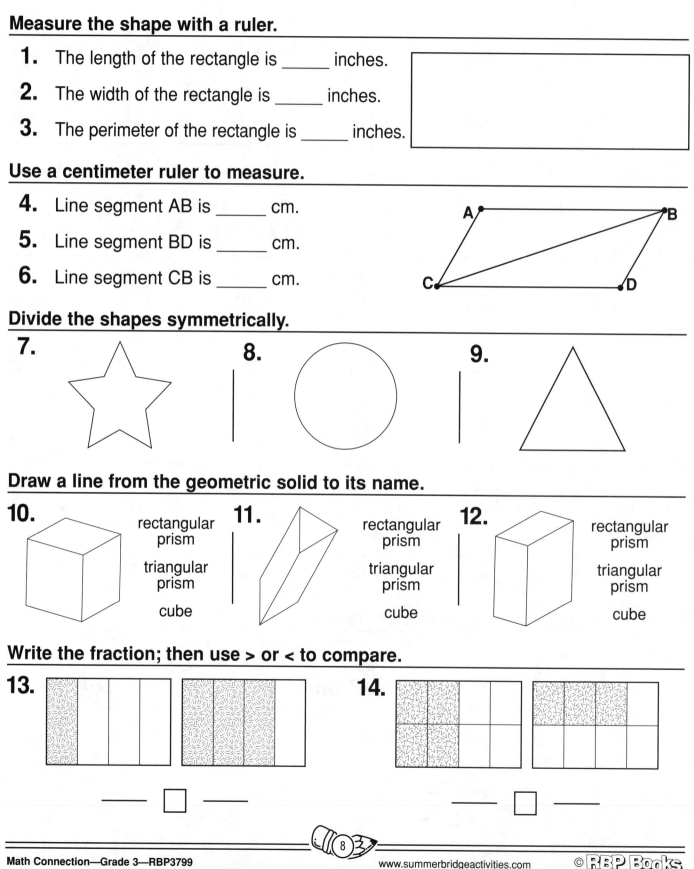

Measure the shape with a ruler.

1. The length of the rectangle is _____ inches.

2. The width of the rectangle is _____ inches.

3. The perimeter of the rectangle is _____ inches.

Use a centimeter ruler to measure.

4. Line segment AB is _____ cm.

5. Line segment BD is _____ cm.

6. Line segment CB is _____ cm.

Divide the shapes symmetrically.

7.   **8.**   **9.**

Draw a line from the geometric solid to its name.

10.
rectangular prism

triangular prism

cube

11.
rectangular prism

triangular prism

cube

12.
rectangular prism

triangular prism

cube

Write the fraction; then use > or < to compare.

13. ____ □ ____

14. ____ □ ____

Diagnostic Test Analysis

After you review your students diagnostic test, match those problems with incorrect answers to the sections below. Pay special attention to the pages that fall into these sections and make sure that your student receives supervision in these areas. In this way, your student will strengthen math skills in these areas.

Addition and Subtraction Facts

Diagnostic Test 1
Problems 1–3
Review Pages:
26–37

Numeration 0–99

Diagnostic Test 1
Problems 4–7
Review Pages:
10–14

Addition and Subtraction of 2-Digit Numbers

Diagnostic Test 2
Problems 1–4
Review Pages:
38–51

Numeration 100–9,999

Diagnostic Test 3
Problems 1–8
Review Pages:
15–25

Addition and Subtraction of Large Numbers

Diagnostic Test 3
Problems 9–12
Review Pages:
52–69

Multiplication and Division Facts

Diagnostic Test 4
Problems 1–4 and 10–12
Review Pages:
89–98, 99–105, 106–109

Multiplication with 2-Digits

Diagnostic Test 4
Problems 5–7
Review Pages:
110–121

Division with Remainders

Diagnostic Test 4
Problems 8–9
Review Pages:
122–28

Telling Time

Diagnostic Test 2
Problems 5–12
Review Pages:
73–77, 85–86

Counting Money

Diagnostic Test 2
Problems 13–15
Review Pages:
78–86

Measurement

Diagnostic Test 5
Problems 1–6
Review Pages:
70–72, 85–86

Geometry

Diagnostic Test 5
Problems 7–12
Review Pages:
129–132

Fractions

Diagnostic Test 5
Problems 13–14
Review Pages:
133–139

Reading Number Words

Write the number.

1.

six   __6__

one _____

three _____

ten _____

seven _____

2.

four _____

two _____

nine _____

five _____

eight _____

3.

thirteen _____

twelve _____

twenty _____

eighteen _____

forty _____

4.

sixteen _____

seventeen _____

eleven _____

thirty _____

fifty _____

5.

sixty-four _____

thirty-one _____

seventy-two _____

twenty-seven _____

eighty-one _____

6.

ninety-eight _____

fifty-three _____

eighty-five _____

forty-six _____

ninety-three _____

Math Connection—Grade 3—RBP3799   www.summerbridgeactivities.com   © RBP Books

Writing Numbers 0–99

Start with 0. Write to 99.

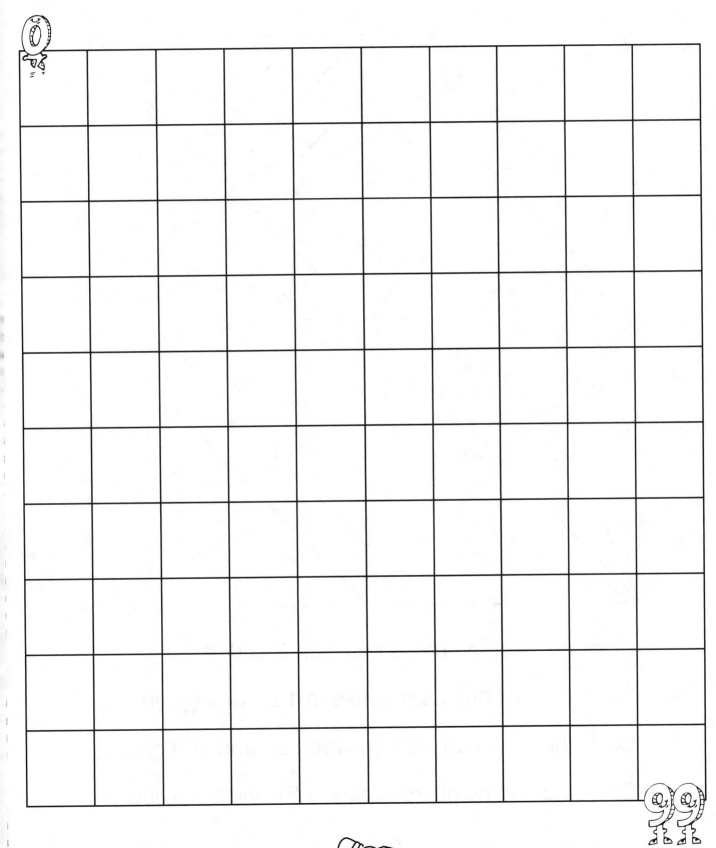

© RBP Books   www.summerbridgeactivities.com   Math Connection—Grade 3—RBP3799

Odd and Even Numbers

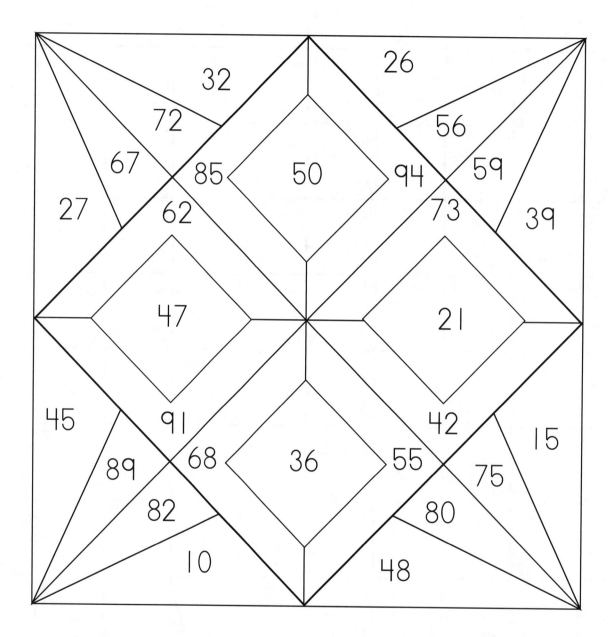

1. Color the even numbers between 2 and 50 <u>blue</u>.

2. Color the odd numbers between 1 and 49 <u>green</u>.

3. Color the even numbers between 52 and 100 <u>orange</u>.

4. Color the odd numbers between 51 and 99 <u>yellow</u>.

Tens and Ones

Write how many tens and ones. Then write the number.

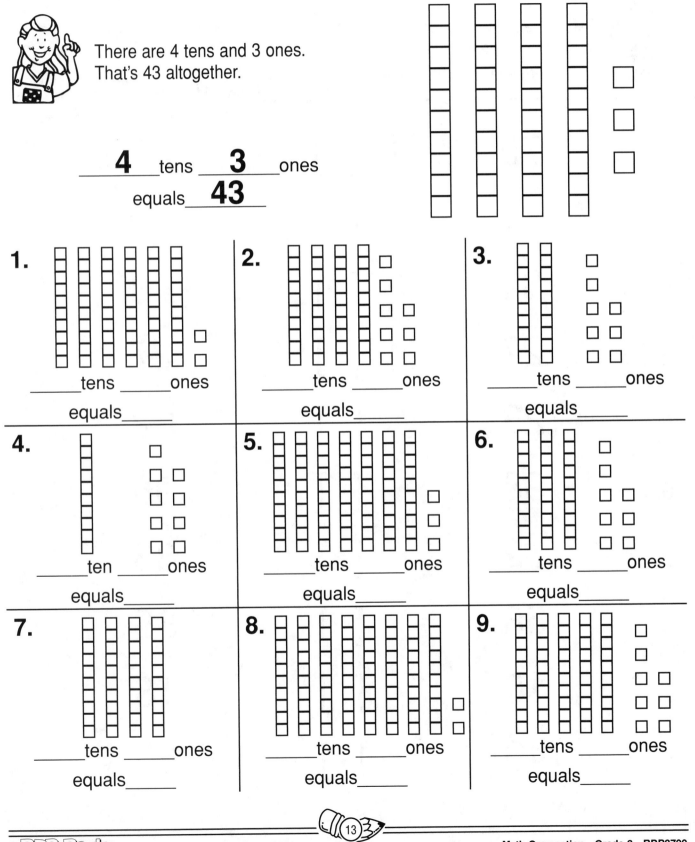

There are 4 tens and 3 ones.
That's 43 altogether.

_____**4**_____ tens _____**3**_____ ones
equals _____**43**_____

1. _____ tens _____ ones

equals _____

2. _____ tens _____ ones

equals _____

3. _____ tens _____ ones

equals _____

4. _____ ten _____ ones

equals _____

5. _____ tens _____ ones

equals _____

6. _____ tens _____ ones

equals _____

7. _____ tens _____ ones

equals _____

8. _____ tens _____ ones

equals _____

9. _____ tens _____ ones

equals _____

www.summerbridgeactivities.com   **Math Connection—Grade 3—RBP3799**

Comparing Numbers

Use >, <, or = to make each problem correct.

Remember, the arrow points to the smaller number and opens wide to the larger number. 64 > 62 means 64 is more than 62.

= means **equal to**

> means **more than**

< means **less than**

1. 72 [ ] 27

2. 61 [ ] 60

3. 34 [ ] 43

4. 27 [ ] 27

5. 23 [ ] 32

6. 98 [ ] 96

7. 82 [ ] 83

8. 56 [ ] 65

9. 18 [ ] 18

10. 49 [ ] 50

Hundreds, Tens, and Ones

Write how many hundreds, tens, and ones. Then write the number.

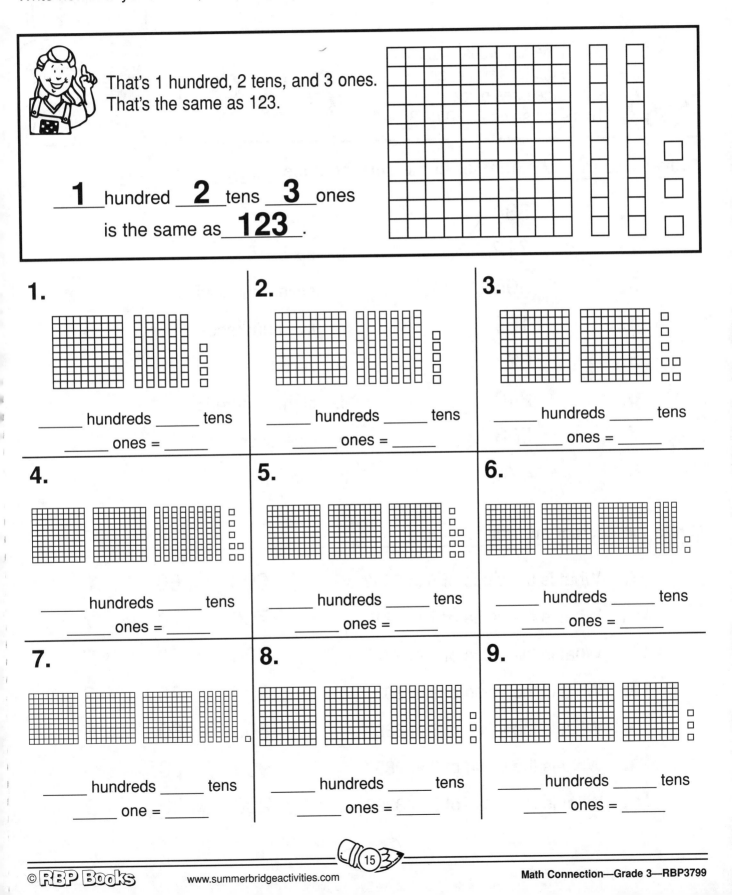

That's 1 hundred, 2 tens, and 3 ones.
That's the same as 123.

__1__ hundred __2__ tens __3__ ones
is the same as __123__.

1.
_____ hundreds _____ tens
_____ ones = _____

2.
_____ hundreds _____ tens
_____ ones = _____

3.
_____ hundreds _____ tens
_____ ones = _____

4.
_____ hundreds _____ tens
_____ ones = _____

5.
_____ hundreds _____ tens
_____ ones = _____

6.
_____ hundreds _____ tens
_____ ones = _____

7.
_____ hundreds _____ tens
_____ one = _____

8.
_____ hundreds _____ tens
_____ ones = _____

9.
_____ hundreds _____ tens
_____ ones = _____

www.summerbridgeactivities.com **Math Connection—Grade 3—RBP3799**

Numbers 100–999

8 is in the hundreds place,
3 is in the tens place, and
9 is in the ones place.
That's the same as 800 + 30 + 9.

8 3 9

Who ordered the 221?

Draw a line from the number to the correct place value.

1.	834	a.	four tens
2.	712	b.	six ones
3.	305	c.	seven hundreds
4.	189	d.	five hundreds
5.	627	e.	zero tens
6.	240	f.	eight hundreds
7.	568	g.	nine ones
8.	476	h.	two tens

Circle the correct answer.

9.	What is the value of 6 in 863?	600	60	6
10.	What is the value of 7 in 721?	700	70	7
11.	What is the value of 7 in 874?	700	70	7
12.	What is the value of 9 in 809?	900	90	9
13.	What is the value of 6 in 639?	600	60	6
14.	What is the value of 9 in 980?	900	90	9
15.	What is the value of 2 in 329?	200	20	2

Math Connection—Grade 3—RBP3799   www.summerbridgeactivities.com   © RBP Books

Reading Numbers 100–999

 This number is seven hundred forty-three.
Don't use the word "**and**"
when writing or saying large numbers.

743

Draw lines to match the number with the number word.

1.	347	a.	five hundred nine
2.	279	b.	nine hundred ninety-nine
3.	960	c.	three hundred forty-seven
4.	719	d.	nine hundred sixty
5.	801	e.	one hundred thirty-five
6.	590	f.	six hundred eighty
7.	135	g.	two hundred seventy-nine
8.	509	h.	seven hundred nineteen
9.	680	i.	eight hundred one
10.	999	j.	five hundred ninety

Write the number that means the same as each number word.

11.	three hundred thirteen	_____
12.	eight hundred nine	_____
13.	four hundred twenty-six	_____
14.	two hundred eleven	_____
15.	seven hundred fifty-one	_____
16.	one hundred five	_____
17.	five hundred thirty-two	_____
18.	nine hundred forty-four	_____

Comparing Numbers 100–999

When comparing numbers, look at the hundreds place first. If the hundreds are the same, then compare the tens and ones.

I ♡ the least and the most equally!

Circle the number that is the least.

1. 173	(149)	156	206	347	165
2. 699	943	943	878	566	903
3. 510	430	530	770	680	820
4. 390	745	845	691	759	425
5. 941	812	852	814	916	804

Circle the number that is the most.

6. 746	981	873	699	990	847
7. 633	709	599	671	433	598
8. 695	768	845	871	555	796
9. 493	561	664	793	990	889
10. 567	765	675	783	623	805

Use greater than (>), less than (<), or equal to (=) to complete each problem.

11. 439 [<] 670   **12.** 944 [ ] 872

13. 730 [ ] 750   **14.** 610 [ ] 610

15. 567 [ ] 576   **16.** 887 [ ] 891

17. 991 [ ] 991   **18.** 499 [ ] 500

19. 635 [ ] 471   **20.** 781 [ ] 902

Thousands, Hundreds, Tens, and Ones

Write how many thousands, hundreds, tens, and ones. Then write the number.

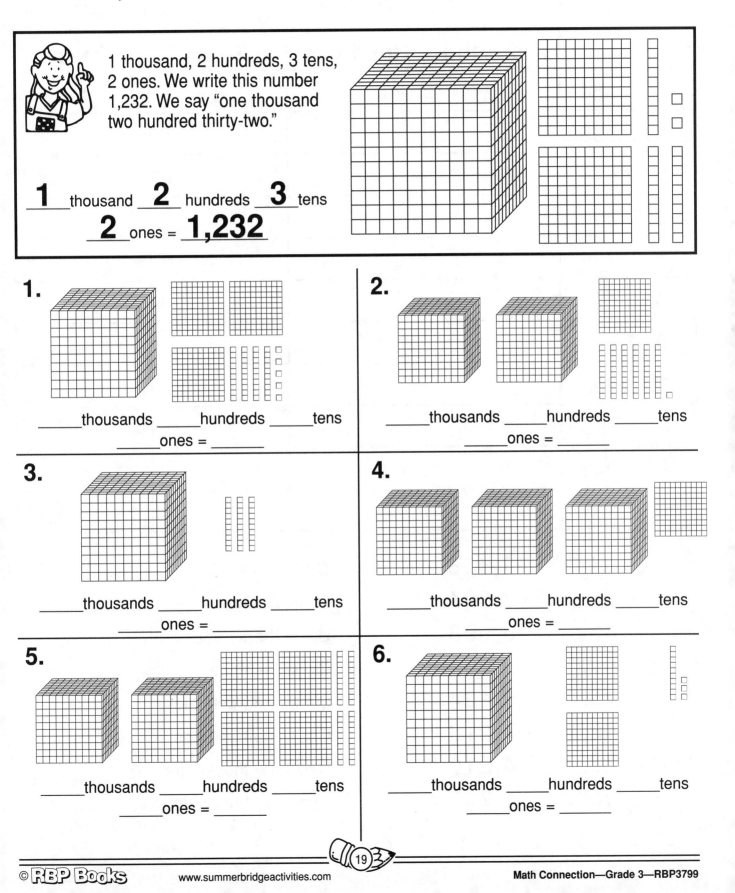

1 thousand, 2 hundreds, 3 tens, 2 ones. We write this number 1,232. We say "one thousand two hundred thirty-two."

__1__ thousand __2__ hundreds __3__ tens
__2__ ones = **1,232**

1.

_____thousands _____hundreds _____tens
_____ones = _____

2.

_____thousands _____hundreds _____tens
_____ones = _____

3.

_____thousands _____hundreds _____tens
_____ones = _____

4.

_____thousands _____hundreds _____tens
_____ones = _____

5.

_____thousands _____hundreds _____tens
_____ones = _____

6.

_____thousands _____hundreds _____tens
_____ones = _____

www.summerbridgeactivities.com   **Math Connection—Grade 3—RBP3799**

Thousands, Hundreds, Tens, and Ones

Write the value of each number.

	Thousands	Hundreds	Tens	Ones
3,464	3	4	6	4
1. 5,739				
2. 4,650				
3. 7,381				
4. 736				
5. 1,475				
6. 5,837				
7. 6,902				
8. 4,560				
9. 1,048				
10. 1,111				

11.	3,4⑤6	Circle the tens.
12.	7,394	Circle the hundreds.
13.	5,098	Circle the thousands.
14.	8,962	Circle the ones.
15.	6,124	Circle the thousands.
16.	7,218	Circle the hundreds.
17.	4,810	Circle the thousands.
18.	1,702	Circle the hundreds.

Math Connection—Grade 3—RBP3799   www.summerbridgeactivities.com   © RBP Books

Expanded Numbers

Write the numeral that means the same.

1. 1,000 + 500 + 30 + 3 = _____**1,533**_____

2. 5,000 + 900 + 40 + 7 = _____

3. 3,000 + 700 + 50 + 5 = _____

4. 7,000 + 400 + 70 + 9 = _____

5. 9,000 + 20 + 1 = _____

6. 3,000 + 100 + 2 = _____

7. 3,000 + 500 + 6 = _____

8. 6,000 + 90 + 8 = _____

9. 3,000 + 600 + 9 = _____

10. 1,000 + 600 + 90 + 8 = _____

Write the number in expanded form.

11. 3,456 _____

12. 7,324 _____

13. 9,152 _____

14. 3,569 _____

15. 2,431 _____

16. 4,022 _____

Reading and Writing Numbers 1,000–9,999

Match the number with the number word.

1.	4,012	six thousand two
2.	4,720	six thousand three hundred sixteen
3.	6,999	four thousand twelve
4.	4,203	four thousand two hundred three
5.	6,002	four thousand seven hundred twenty
6.	6,316	six thousand nine hundred ninety-nine

Write the number.

7.	Three thousand four hundred sixteen	**3,416**
8.	Nine thousand three hundred fifty	_____
9.	Seven thousand twenty-one	_____
10.	One thousand five hundred ninety-two	_____
11.	Four thousand two hundred six	_____
12.	Nine thousand nine hundred ninety-nine	_____

Write the number.

13.	3,396	**three thousand three hundred ninety-six**
14.	4,553	_____
15.	8,056	_____
16.	3,621	_____
17.	7,250	_____
18.	3,302	_____

Math Connection—Grade 3—RBP3799   www.summerbridgeactivities.com   © RBP Books

Comparing Numbers

2,980 [>] 2,976

To compare numbers, I look at the thousands place. 2,000 and 2,000 are equal, so I look at the hundreds place. 900 and 900 are equal, so I look at the tens place. 80 is greater than 70, so 2,980 is greater than (>) 2,976.

Use greater than (>) or less than (<) to tell about the numbers.

1.	3,496	[ ]	3,340	**2.**	7,325	[ ]	9,468
3.	3,745	[ ]	3,739	**4.**	6,478	[ ]	6,502
5.	8,376	[ ]	9,257	**6.**	3,581	[ ]	3,576
7.	7,943	[ ]	6,293	**8.**	5,030	[ ]	4,997
9.	5,429	[ ]	6,124	**10.**	4,927	[ ]	4,866

Write the numbers in order from the least to the greatest.

11. 70,459   52,763   49,377   51,790   73,210

_____   _____   _____   _____   _____
least   greatest

12. 120,725   112,948   241,350   326,291   111,997

_____   _____   _____   _____   _____
least   greatest

Write the numbers in order from the greatest to the least.

13. 3,463   5,927   2,944   7,205   6,249

_____   _____   _____   _____   _____
greatest   least

14. 8,516   21,050   18,293   17,356   22,341

_____   _____   _____   _____   _____
greatest   least

www.summerbridgeactivities.com   Math Connection—Grade 3—RBP3799

Numeration Assessment

Write the number words.

1. 27 _____   **2.** 346 _____

3. 59 _____   **4.** 108 _____

5. 9,213 _____

Write the number.

6. thirty-four _____   **7.** five hundred sixteen _____

8. sixty-one _____   **9.** seven hundred eighty _____

10. two thousand nine hundred ninety-two _____

Circle the correct answer.

11. What is the value of 2 in 210?   2   20   200

12. What is the value of 4 in 841?   4   40   400

13. What is the value of 7 in 5,037?   7   70   700

Use greater than (>), less than (<), or equal to (=) to complete each problem.

14. 43 $\bigcirc$ 34   **15.** 67 $\bigcirc$ 76

16. 127 $\bigcirc$ 171   **17.** 390 $\bigcirc$ 309

18. 7,893 $\bigcirc$ 7,983   **19.** 4,999 $\bigcirc$ 3,999

Arrange the numbers in order from the least to the greatest.

20.   230   610   804   517   429

_____ _____ _____ _____ _____
least   greatest

Arrange the numbers in order from the greatest to the least.

21.   7,380   7,378   7,197   7,382   7,391

_____ _____ _____ _____ _____
greatest   least

Write the number.

22. $300 + 60 + 8 =$ _____   **23.** $4,000 + 200 + 10 + 5 =$ _____

Write the number in expanded form.

24. 648 _____

25. 1,529 _____

Numeration Assessment

Write the number words.

1. 31 _____

2. 64 _____

3. 219 _____

4. 507 _____

5. 8,390 _____

Write the number.

6. twenty-three _____

7. four hundred fifty-two _____

8. seventy-eight _____

9. six hundred eighty-seven _____

10. three thousand seventeen _____

Circle the correct answer.

11.	What is the value of 3 in 230?	3	30	300
12.	What is the value of 1 in 721?	1	10	100
13.	What is the value of 5 in 5,923?	50	500	5000

Use greater than (>), less than (<), or equal to (=) to complete each problem.

14.	23 ◯ 32	**15.**	88 ◯ 86
16.	393 ◯ 339	**17.**	701 ◯ 710
18.	2,000 ◯ 1,999	**19.**	8,327 ◯ 8,372

Arrange the numbers in order from the least to the greatest.

20.   739   793   937   379   397

_____ _____ _____ _____ _____
least   greatest

Arrange the numbers in order from the greatest to the least.

21.   4,820   4,819   4,825   4,802   4,189

_____ _____ _____ _____ _____
least   greatest

Write the number.

22. 500 + 90 + 6 = _____

23. 3,000 + 100 + 70 + 6 = _____

Write the number in expanded notation.

24. 902 _____

25. 8,821 _____

Addition Facts 0–18

Write the sum.

> Think about the number families.
> Try to learn these facts.

1. $\begin{array}{r}2\\+\,2\\\hline \mathbf{4}\end{array}$ $\begin{array}{r}6\\+\,3\\\hline\end{array}$ $\begin{array}{r}4\\+\,5\\\hline\end{array}$ $\begin{array}{r}2\\+\,6\\\hline\end{array}$ $\begin{array}{r}4\\+\,6\\\hline\end{array}$ $\begin{array}{r}3\\+\,9\\\hline\end{array}$

2. $\begin{array}{r}6\\+\,7\\\hline\end{array}$ $\begin{array}{r}5\\+\,2\\\hline\end{array}$ $\begin{array}{r}2\\+\,3\\\hline\end{array}$ $\begin{array}{r}4\\+\,3\\\hline\end{array}$ $\begin{array}{r}9\\+\,9\\\hline\end{array}$ $\begin{array}{r}4\\+\,9\\\hline\end{array}$

3. $\begin{array}{r}2\\+\,7\\\hline\end{array}$ $\begin{array}{r}3\\+\,5\\\hline\end{array}$ $\begin{array}{r}9\\+\,7\\\hline\end{array}$ $\begin{array}{r}5\\+\,8\\\hline\end{array}$ $\begin{array}{r}6\\+\,9\\\hline\end{array}$ $\begin{array}{r}4\\+\,2\\\hline\end{array}$

4. $\begin{array}{r}4\\+\,4\\\hline\end{array}$ $\begin{array}{r}5\\+\,5\\\hline\end{array}$ $\begin{array}{r}7\\+\,4\\\hline\end{array}$ $\begin{array}{r}7\\+\,7\\\hline\end{array}$ $\begin{array}{r}6\\+\,5\\\hline\end{array}$ $\begin{array}{r}5\\+\,7\\\hline\end{array}$

5. $\begin{array}{r}8\\+\,4\\\hline\end{array}$ $\begin{array}{r}7\\+\,8\\\hline\end{array}$ $\begin{array}{r}7\\+\,3\\\hline\end{array}$ $\begin{array}{r}9\\+\,2\\\hline\end{array}$ $\begin{array}{r}8\\+\,8\\\hline\end{array}$ $\begin{array}{r}8\\+\,2\\\hline\end{array}$

6. $\begin{array}{r}3\\+\,3\\\hline\end{array}$ $\begin{array}{r}9\\+\,5\\\hline\end{array}$ $\begin{array}{r}9\\+\,8\\\hline\end{array}$ $\begin{array}{r}6\\+\,6\\\hline\end{array}$ $\begin{array}{r}8\\+\,3\\\hline\end{array}$ $\begin{array}{r}8\\+\,6\\\hline\end{array}$

Math Connection—Grade 3—RBP3799   www.summerbridgeactivities.com   © RBP Books

Name _____ Date _____

Addition Facts 0–18

Write the sum.

Make some flash cards to study the
facts you have trouble remembering.

1.
$\begin{array}{r} 3 \\ + 7 \\ \hline \mathbf{10} \end{array}$
$\begin{array}{r} 4 \\ + 6 \\ \hline \end{array}$
$\begin{array}{r} 2 \\ + 5 \\ \hline \end{array}$
$\begin{array}{r} 1 \\ + 7 \\ \hline \end{array}$
$\begin{array}{r} 8 \\ + 4 \\ \hline \end{array}$
$\begin{array}{r} 2 \\ + 9 \\ \hline \end{array}$

2.
$\begin{array}{r} 5 \\ + 1 \\ \hline \end{array}$
$\begin{array}{r} 7 \\ + 2 \\ \hline \end{array}$
$\begin{array}{r} 8 \\ + 9 \\ \hline \end{array}$
$\begin{array}{r} 2 \\ + 6 \\ \hline \end{array}$
$\begin{array}{r} 3 \\ + 4 \\ \hline \end{array}$
$\begin{array}{r} 5 \\ + 7 \\ \hline \end{array}$

3.
$\begin{array}{r} 6 \\ + 6 \\ \hline \end{array}$
$\begin{array}{r} 8 \\ + 5 \\ \hline \end{array}$
$\begin{array}{r} 7 \\ + 9 \\ \hline \end{array}$
$\begin{array}{r} 3 \\ + 8 \\ \hline \end{array}$
$\begin{array}{r} 2 \\ + 4 \\ \hline \end{array}$
$\begin{array}{r} 9 \\ + 3 \\ \hline \end{array}$

4.
$\begin{array}{r} 4 \\ + 5 \\ \hline \end{array}$
$\begin{array}{r} 7 \\ + 7 \\ \hline \end{array}$
$\begin{array}{r} 5 \\ + 8 \\ \hline \end{array}$
$\begin{array}{r} 6 \\ + 7 \\ \hline \end{array}$
$\begin{array}{r} 8 \\ + 8 \\ \hline \end{array}$
$\begin{array}{r} 9 \\ + 6 \\ \hline \end{array}$

5.
$\begin{array}{r} 7 \\ + 8 \\ \hline \end{array}$
$\begin{array}{r} 6 \\ + 5 \\ \hline \end{array}$
$\begin{array}{r} 4 \\ + 9 \\ \hline \end{array}$
$\begin{array}{r} 8 \\ + 3 \\ \hline \end{array}$
$\begin{array}{r} 4 \\ + 4 \\ \hline \end{array}$
$\begin{array}{r} 9 \\ + 5 \\ \hline \end{array}$

6.
$\begin{array}{r} 9 \\ + 9 \\ \hline \end{array}$
$\begin{array}{r} 9 \\ + 7 \\ \hline \end{array}$
$\begin{array}{r} 6 \\ + 4 \\ \hline \end{array}$
$\begin{array}{r} 7 \\ + 6 \\ \hline \end{array}$
$\begin{array}{r} 9 \\ + 8 \\ \hline \end{array}$
$\begin{array}{r} 8 \\ + 7 \\ \hline \end{array}$

www.summerbridgeactivities.com Math Connection—Grade 3—RBP3799

Column Addition

Solve each problem.

Add the first two numbers.	4
Then add the sum of the	3
first two to the last number.	+ 7
4 plus 3 equals 7. 7 plus 7 equals 14.	**14**

1.

1	4	3	7	2	1	6
3	2	4	1	8	9	5
+ 2	+ 1	+ 2	+ 2	+ 1	+ 1	+ 1

2.

3	3	7	4	2	5	3
5	6	2	3	2	3	7
+ 4	+ 1	+ 4	+ 7	+ 3	+ 2	+ 2

3.

2	6	4	5	7	9	8
8	4	4	5	7	4	7
+ 3	+ 3	+ 3	+ 5	+ 3	+ 1	+ 3

4.

5	4	2	7	8	6	3
3	8	9	5	2	2	3
4	2	1	3	5	2	4
+ 1	+ 1	+ 3	+ 3	+ 3	+ 8	+ 3

5.

3	4	9	6	7	8	1
7	8	1	6	8	3	8
5	2	5	3	1	0	2
+ 1	+ 3	+ 2	+ 3	+ 2	+ 2	+ 7

Math Connection—Grade 3—RBP3799   www.summerbridgeactivities.com   © RBP Books

Subtraction Facts 0–18

Write the difference.

Keep practicing until you
know these facts.

1.
$$\begin{array}{r} 12 \\ -\ 8 \\ \hline \mathbf{4} \end{array}$$
$$\begin{array}{r} 8 \\ -\ 2 \\ \hline \end{array}$$
$$\begin{array}{r} 9 \\ -\ 2 \\ \hline \end{array}$$
$$\begin{array}{r} 13 \\ -\ 6 \\ \hline \end{array}$$
$$\begin{array}{r} 11 \\ -\ 8 \\ \hline \end{array}$$
$$\begin{array}{r} 14 \\ -\ 5 \\ \hline \end{array}$$

2.
$$\begin{array}{r} 8 \\ -\ 5 \\ \hline \end{array}$$
$$\begin{array}{r} 13 \\ -\ 9 \\ \hline \end{array}$$
$$\begin{array}{r} 10 \\ -\ 6 \\ \hline \end{array}$$
$$\begin{array}{r} 9 \\ -\ 5 \\ \hline \end{array}$$
$$\begin{array}{r} 7 \\ -\ 4 \\ \hline \end{array}$$
$$\begin{array}{r} 13 \\ -\ 5 \\ \hline \end{array}$$

3.
$$\begin{array}{r} 14 \\ -\ 8 \\ \hline \end{array}$$
$$\begin{array}{r} 16 \\ -\ 8 \\ \hline \end{array}$$
$$\begin{array}{r} 12 \\ -\ 7 \\ \hline \end{array}$$
$$\begin{array}{r} 11 \\ -\ 2 \\ \hline \end{array}$$
$$\begin{array}{r} 4 \\ -\ 2 \\ \hline \end{array}$$
$$\begin{array}{r} 15 \\ -\ 9 \\ \hline \end{array}$$

4.
$$\begin{array}{r} 10 \\ -\ 7 \\ \hline \end{array}$$
$$\begin{array}{r} 11 \\ -\ 6 \\ \hline \end{array}$$
$$\begin{array}{r} 6 \\ -\ 3 \\ \hline \end{array}$$
$$\begin{array}{r} 12 \\ -\ 3 \\ \hline \end{array}$$
$$\begin{array}{r} 9 \\ -\ 6 \\ \hline \end{array}$$
$$\begin{array}{r} 12 \\ -\ 6 \\ \hline \end{array}$$

5.
$$\begin{array}{r} 13 \\ -\ 8 \\ \hline \end{array}$$
$$\begin{array}{r} 10 \\ -\ 2 \\ \hline \end{array}$$
$$\begin{array}{r} 16 \\ -\ 9 \\ \hline \end{array}$$
$$\begin{array}{r} 10 \\ -\ 5 \\ \hline \end{array}$$
$$\begin{array}{r} 17 \\ -\ 8 \\ \hline \end{array}$$
$$\begin{array}{r} 11 \\ -\ 4 \\ \hline \end{array}$$

6.
$$\begin{array}{r} 18 \\ -\ 9 \\ \hline \end{array}$$
$$\begin{array}{r} 8 \\ -\ 4 \\ \hline \end{array}$$
$$\begin{array}{r} 14 \\ -\ 7 \\ \hline \end{array}$$
$$\begin{array}{r} 15 \\ -\ 7 \\ \hline \end{array}$$
$$\begin{array}{r} 5 \\ -\ 2 \\ \hline \end{array}$$
$$\begin{array}{r} 6 \\ -\ 4 \\ \hline \end{array}$$

Subtraction Facts 0–18

Write the difference.

Memorizing the addition and subtraction facts will help you as you learn harder math.

1.
$$\begin{array}{r} 17 \\ -\ 9 \\ \hline \mathbf{8} \end{array}\qquad \begin{array}{r} 13 \\ -\ 7 \\ \hline \end{array}\qquad \begin{array}{r} 15 \\ -\ 7 \\ \hline \end{array}\qquad \begin{array}{r} 12 \\ -\ 5 \\ \hline \end{array}\qquad \begin{array}{r} 10 \\ -\ 3 \\ \hline \end{array}\qquad \begin{array}{r} 6 \\ -\ 2 \\ \hline \end{array}$$

2.
$$\begin{array}{r} 16 \\ -\ 7 \\ \hline \end{array}\qquad \begin{array}{r} 14 \\ -\ 6 \\ \hline \end{array}\qquad \begin{array}{r} 11 \\ -\ 9 \\ \hline \end{array}\qquad \begin{array}{r} 8 \\ -\ 6 \\ \hline \end{array}\qquad \begin{array}{r} 7 \\ -\ 3 \\ \hline \end{array}\qquad \begin{array}{r} 17 \\ -\ 8 \\ \hline \end{array}$$

3.
$$\begin{array}{r} 15 \\ -\ 8 \\ \hline \end{array}\qquad \begin{array}{r} 12 \\ -\ 9 \\ \hline \end{array}\qquad \begin{array}{r} 9 \\ -\ 5 \\ \hline \end{array}\qquad \begin{array}{r} 11 \\ -\ 6 \\ \hline \end{array}\qquad \begin{array}{r} 13 \\ -\ 8 \\ \hline \end{array}\qquad \begin{array}{r} 8 \\ -\ 5 \\ \hline \end{array}$$

4.
$$\begin{array}{r} 14 \\ -\ 9 \\ \hline \end{array}\qquad \begin{array}{r} 7 \\ -\ 5 \\ \hline \end{array}\qquad \begin{array}{r} 12 \\ -\ 4 \\ \hline \end{array}\qquad \begin{array}{r} 5 \\ -\ 3 \\ \hline \end{array}\qquad \begin{array}{r} 11 \\ -\ 3 \\ \hline \end{array}\qquad \begin{array}{r} 18 \\ -\ 9 \\ \hline \end{array}$$

5.
$$\begin{array}{r} 13 \\ -\ 4 \\ \hline \end{array}\qquad \begin{array}{r} 10 \\ -\ 8 \\ \hline \end{array}\qquad \begin{array}{r} 9 \\ -\ 7 \\ \hline \end{array}\qquad \begin{array}{r} 12 \\ -\ 3 \\ \hline \end{array}\qquad \begin{array}{r} 14 \\ -\ 7 \\ \hline \end{array}\qquad \begin{array}{r} 16 \\ -\ 9 \\ \hline \end{array}$$

6.
$$\begin{array}{r} 15 \\ -\ 6 \\ \hline \end{array}\qquad \begin{array}{r} 12 \\ -\ 7 \\ \hline \end{array}\qquad \begin{array}{r} 13 \\ -\ 5 \\ \hline \end{array}\qquad \begin{array}{r} 11 \\ -\ 8 \\ \hline \end{array}\qquad \begin{array}{r} 16 \\ -\ 8 \\ \hline \end{array}\qquad \begin{array}{r} 14 \\ -\ 8 \\ \hline \end{array}$$

Addition and Subtraction Practice 0–18

Solve each problem.

Watch the signs.

Keep your eyes open for those tricky signs!

1.
$\begin{array}{r} 2 \\ + 3 \\ \hline \end{array}$
$\begin{array}{r} 5 \\ + 2 \\ \hline \end{array}$
$\begin{array}{r} 11 \\ - 6 \\ \hline \end{array}$
$\begin{array}{r} 6 \\ - 4 \\ \hline \end{array}$
$\begin{array}{r} 12 \\ - 4 \\ \hline \end{array}$
$\begin{array}{r} 8 \\ + 3 \\ \hline \end{array}$

2.
$\begin{array}{r} 8 \\ + 7 \\ \hline \end{array}$
$\begin{array}{r} 11 \\ - 4 \\ \hline \end{array}$
$\begin{array}{r} 9 \\ + 2 \\ \hline \end{array}$
$\begin{array}{r} 6 \\ + 8 \\ \hline \end{array}$
$\begin{array}{r} 10 \\ - 5 \\ \hline \end{array}$
$\begin{array}{r} 7 \\ + 7 \\ \hline \end{array}$

3.
$\begin{array}{r} 2 \\ + 2 \\ \hline \end{array}$
$\begin{array}{r} 9 \\ + 4 \\ \hline \end{array}$
$\begin{array}{r} 3 \\ + 6 \\ \hline \end{array}$
$\begin{array}{r} 10 \\ - 7 \\ \hline \end{array}$
$\begin{array}{r} 8 \\ + 2 \\ \hline \end{array}$
$\begin{array}{r} 8 \\ + 5 \\ \hline \end{array}$

4.
$\begin{array}{r} 3 \\ + 3 \\ \hline \end{array}$
$\begin{array}{r} 13 \\ - 7 \\ \hline \end{array}$
$\begin{array}{r} 2 \\ + 6 \\ \hline \end{array}$
$\begin{array}{r} 14 \\ - 5 \\ \hline \end{array}$
$\begin{array}{r} 6 \\ + 6 \\ \hline \end{array}$
$\begin{array}{r} 4 \\ + 4 \\ \hline \end{array}$

5.
$\begin{array}{r} 6 \\ + 9 \\ \hline \end{array}$
$\begin{array}{r} 2 \\ + 7 \\ \hline \end{array}$
$\begin{array}{r} 8 \\ + 9 \\ \hline \end{array}$
$\begin{array}{r} 12 \\ - 9 \\ \hline \end{array}$
$\begin{array}{r} 7 \\ - 4 \\ \hline \end{array}$
$\begin{array}{r} 9 \\ + 9 \\ \hline \end{array}$

6.
$\begin{array}{r} 9 \\ - 5 \\ \hline \end{array}$
$\begin{array}{r} 16 \\ - 8 \\ \hline \end{array}$
$\begin{array}{r} 12 \\ - 7 \\ \hline \end{array}$
$\begin{array}{r} 3 \\ + 5 \\ \hline \end{array}$
$\begin{array}{r} 9 \\ + 7 \\ \hline \end{array}$
$\begin{array}{r} 6 \\ + 4 \\ \hline \end{array}$

Addition and Subtraction Practice 0–18

Solve each problem.

 Write the answers to these problems on another sheet of paper. Time yourself as you do the problems. Do the problems again. Try to improve your time.

1.
$\begin{array}{r} 4 \\ +\ 8 \\ \hline \mathbf{12} \end{array}$
$\begin{array}{r} 5 \\ +\ 6 \\ \hline \end{array}$
$\begin{array}{r} 12 \\ -\ 5 \\ \hline \end{array}$
$\begin{array}{r} 11 \\ -\ 7 \\ \hline \end{array}$
$\begin{array}{r} 7 \\ +\ 8 \\ \hline \end{array}$
$\begin{array}{r} 18 \\ -\ 9 \\ \hline \end{array}$

2.
$\begin{array}{r} 9 \\ +\ 6 \\ \hline \end{array}$
$\begin{array}{r} 11 \\ -\ 5 \\ \hline \end{array}$
$\begin{array}{r} 13 \\ -\ 6 \\ \hline \end{array}$
$\begin{array}{r} 3 \\ +\ 9 \\ \hline \end{array}$
$\begin{array}{r} 5 \\ +\ 9 \\ \hline \end{array}$
$\begin{array}{r} 17 \\ -\ 8 \\ \hline \end{array}$

3.
$\begin{array}{r} 4 \\ +\ 3 \\ \hline \end{array}$
$\begin{array}{r} 7 \\ +\ 4 \\ \hline \end{array}$
$\begin{array}{r} 9 \\ +\ 2 \\ \hline \end{array}$
$\begin{array}{r} 12 \\ -\ 6 \\ \hline \end{array}$
$\begin{array}{r} 10 \\ -\ 7 \\ \hline \end{array}$
$\begin{array}{r} 9 \\ -\ 5 \\ \hline \end{array}$

4.
$\begin{array}{r} 12 \\ -\ 9 \\ \hline \end{array}$
$\begin{array}{r} 5 \\ +\ 8 \\ \hline \end{array}$
$\begin{array}{r} 11 \\ -\ 8 \\ \hline \end{array}$
$\begin{array}{r} 6 \\ +\ 7 \\ \hline \end{array}$
$\begin{array}{r} 14 \\ -\ 9 \\ \hline \end{array}$
$\begin{array}{r} 8 \\ +\ 7 \\ \hline \end{array}$

5.
$\begin{array}{r} 15 \\ -\ 9 \\ \hline \end{array}$
$\begin{array}{r} 13 \\ -\ 8 \\ \hline \end{array}$
$\begin{array}{r} 8 \\ -\ 5 \\ \hline \end{array}$
$\begin{array}{r} 7 \\ +\ 5 \\ \hline \end{array}$
$\begin{array}{r} 3 \\ +\ 8 \\ \hline \end{array}$
$\begin{array}{r} 11 \\ -\ 6 \\ \hline \end{array}$

6.
$\begin{array}{r} 8 \\ +\ 9 \\ \hline \end{array}$
$\begin{array}{r} 12 \\ -\ 4 \\ \hline \end{array}$
$\begin{array}{r} 13 \\ -\ 9 \\ \hline \end{array}$
$\begin{array}{r} 7 \\ +\ 7 \\ \hline \end{array}$
$\begin{array}{r} 13 \\ -\ 8 \\ \hline \end{array}$
$\begin{array}{r} 8 \\ +\ 8 \\ \hline \end{array}$

Addition and Subtraction Connection

Solve each problem.

Learning number families helps you learn the number facts.

1. 3 + 4 = ___   7 − 3 = ___   4 + 3 = ___   7 − 4 = ___

2. 6 + 9 = ___   15 − 6 = ___   9 + 6 = ___   15 − 9 = ___

3. 5 + 8 = ___   13 − 5 = ___   8 + 5 = ___   13 − 8 = ___

4. 7 + 4 = ___   11 − 7 = ___   4 + 7 = ___   11 − 4 = ___

5. 6 + 8 = ___   14 − 6 = ___   8 + 6 = ___   14 − 8 = ___

6. 5 + 7 = ___   12 − 5 = ___   7 + 5 = ___   12 − 7 = ___

Write the equations for each number family.

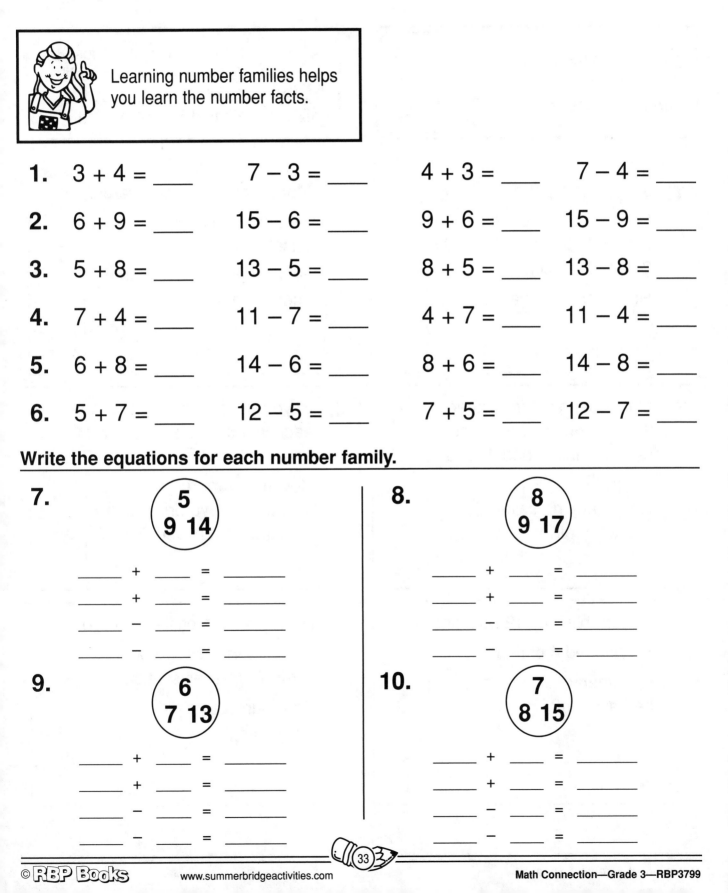

7.   (5 / 9 14)

___ + ___ = ___
___ + ___ = ___
___ − ___ = ___
___ − ___ = ___

8.   (8 / 9 17)

___ + ___ = ___
___ + ___ = ___
___ − ___ = ___
___ − ___ = ___

9.   (6 / 7 13)

___ + ___ = ___
___ + ___ = ___
___ − ___ = ___
___ − ___ = ___

10.   (7 / 8 15)

___ + ___ = ___
___ + ___ = ___
___ − ___ = ___
___ − ___ = ___

Addition and Subtraction Problem Solving

Solve the problems. Do your work in the box. Write your answer on the line.

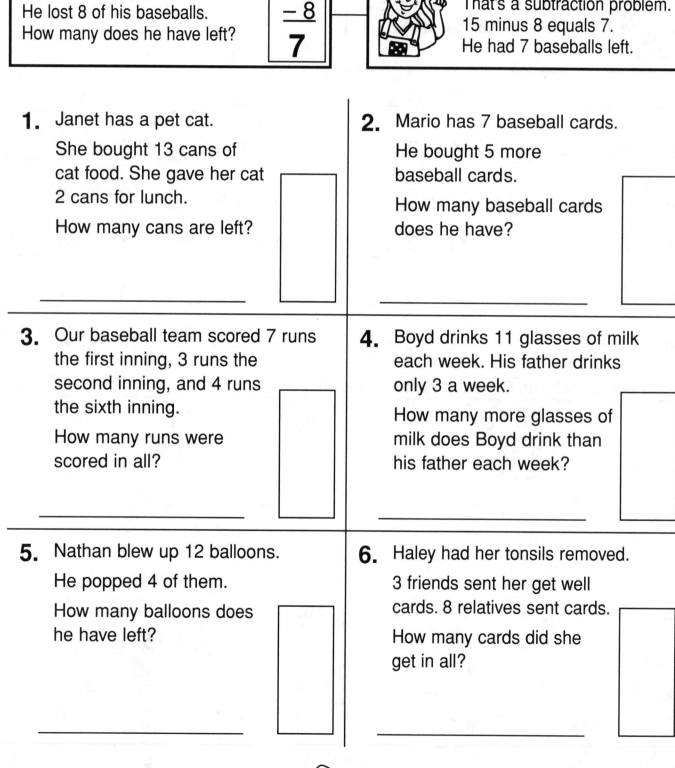

Chris had 15 baseballs.
He lost 8 of his baseballs.
How many does he have left?

$$15 - 8 = 7$$

He had 15 in all. He lost 8.
That's a subtraction problem.
15 minus 8 equals 7.
He had 7 baseballs left.

1. Janet has a pet cat.

She bought 13 cans of cat food. She gave her cat 2 cans for lunch.

How many cans are left?

2. Mario has 7 baseball cards.

He bought 5 more baseball cards.

How many baseball cards does he have?

3. Our baseball team scored 7 runs the first inning, 3 runs the second inning, and 4 runs the sixth inning.

How many runs were scored in all?

4. Boyd drinks 11 glasses of milk each week. His father drinks only 3 a week.

How many more glasses of milk does Boyd drink than his father each week?

5. Nathan blew up 12 balloons.

He popped 4 of them.

How many balloons does he have left?

6. Haley had her tonsils removed.

3 friends sent her get well cards. 8 relatives sent cards.

How many cards did she get in all?

Name _____ Date _____

Addition and Subtraction Problem Solving

Solve the problems. Do your work in the box. Write your answer on the line.

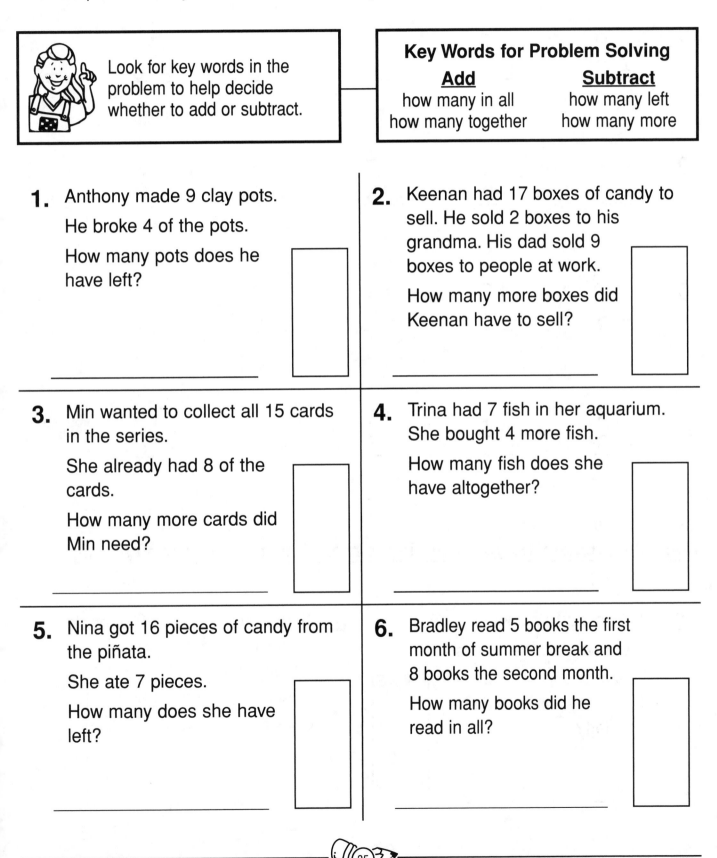

Look for key words in the problem to help decide whether to add or subtract.

Key Words for Problem Solving

Add	Subtract
how many in all	how many left
how many together	how many more

1. Anthony made 9 clay pots.

He broke 4 of the pots.

How many pots does he have left?

2. Keenan had 17 boxes of candy to sell. He sold 2 boxes to his grandma. His dad sold 9 boxes to people at work.

How many more boxes did Keenan have to sell?

3. Min wanted to collect all 15 cards in the series.

She already had 8 of the cards.

How many more cards did Min need?

4. Trina had 7 fish in her aquarium. She bought 4 more fish.

How many fish does she have altogether?

5. Nina got 16 pieces of candy from the piñata.

She ate 7 pieces.

How many does she have left?

6. Bradley read 5 books the first month of summer break and 8 books the second month.

How many books did he read in all?

Addition and Subtraction Assessment
Solve the problems.

1.
$$\begin{array}{r} 9 \\ +\ 3 \\ \hline \end{array}\qquad \begin{array}{r} 7 \\ +\ 2 \\ \hline \end{array}\qquad \begin{array}{r} 4 \\ +\ 8 \\ \hline \end{array}\qquad \begin{array}{r} 1 \\ +\ 9 \\ \hline \end{array}\qquad \begin{array}{r} 6 \\ +\ 6 \\ \hline \end{array}\qquad \begin{array}{r} 5 \\ +\ 4 \\ \hline \end{array}$$

2.
$$\begin{array}{r} 8 \\ +\ 5 \\ \hline \end{array}\qquad \begin{array}{r} 4 \\ +\ 9 \\ \hline \end{array}\qquad \begin{array}{r} 7 \\ +\ 5 \\ \hline \end{array}\qquad \begin{array}{r} 5 \\ +\ 5 \\ \hline \end{array}\qquad \begin{array}{r} 8 \\ +\ 3 \\ \hline \end{array}\qquad \begin{array}{r} 9 \\ +\ 9 \\ \hline \end{array}$$

3.
$$\begin{array}{r} 17 \\ -\ 8 \\ \hline \end{array}\qquad \begin{array}{r} 15 \\ -\ 7 \\ \hline \end{array}\qquad \begin{array}{r} 16 \\ -\ 8 \\ \hline \end{array}\qquad \begin{array}{r} 13 \\ -\ 6 \\ \hline \end{array}\qquad \begin{array}{r} 18 \\ -\ 9 \\ \hline \end{array}\qquad \begin{array}{r} 14 \\ -\ 8 \\ \hline \end{array}$$

4.
$$\begin{array}{r} 15 \\ -\ 9 \\ \hline \end{array}\qquad \begin{array}{r} 14 \\ -\ 7 \\ \hline \end{array}\qquad \begin{array}{r} 13 \\ -\ 5 \\ \hline \end{array}\qquad \begin{array}{r} 12 \\ -\ 8 \\ \hline \end{array}\qquad \begin{array}{r} 17 \\ -\ 9 \\ \hline \end{array}\qquad \begin{array}{r} 15 \\ -\ 6 \\ \hline \end{array}$$

Solve the problem. Do your work in the box. Write your answer on the line.

5. Hallie's cat had 7 kittens.

She gave 5 of the kittens away.

How many kittens did she have left?

_____

6. Tyler read 9 pages of his book yesterday and 8 more pages today.

How many pages of his book has Tyler read?

_____

Math Connection—Grade 3—RBP3799   www.summerbridgeactivities.com   © RBP Books

Addition and Subtraction Assessment

Solve the problems.

1.
8	9	5	4	7	3
+ 3	+ 4	+ 8	+ 9	+ 6	+ 7

2.
7	3	8	5	8	8
+ 5	+ 9	+ 5	+ 5	+ 6	+ 9

3.
16	14	15	14	17	13
− 8	− 7	− 8	− 6	− 9	− 8

4.
14	14	12	12	17	13
− 9	− 6	− 5	− 9	− 8	− 6

Solve the problem. Do your work in the box. Write your answer on the line.

5. Jason has 7 cousins that are girls and 8 cousins that are boys.

   How many cousins does Jason have?

6. Riley has 13 cousins.

   Eight of Riley's cousins are boys.

   How many are girls?

2-Digit Addition

Solve each problem.

Add the ones first.
5 plus 3 equals 8.
Then add the tens.
2 plus 1 equals 3.

25
+ 13
38

This should be a piece of cake for a genius like you!

1.
23
+ 42

64
+ 25

47
+ 31

13
+ 45

55
+ 30

16
+ 53

2.
70
+ 29

82
+ 11

74
+ 23

58
+ 41

26
+ 33

35
+ 54

3.
12
+ 77

83
+ 13

41
+ 37

19
+ 60

22
+ 37

36
+ 23

4.
15
+ 72

18
+ 81

84
+ 12

27
+ 62

46
+ 41

20
+ 51

5.
52
+ 36

75
+ 10

24
+ 43

51
+ 27

29
+ 50

25
+ 61

6.
31
+ 55

47
+ 32

19
+ 30

62
+ 37

33
+ 52

43
+ 31

Math Connection—Grade 3—RBP3799

www.summerbridgeactivities.com

2-Digit Addition

Solve each problem.

 See how knowing your basic math facts makes harder math easier?

1.
```
   34        28        81        54        84        17
 + 15      + 31      + 17      + 35      + 12      + 32
 ----
   49
```

2.
```
   51        73        14        20        41        36
 + 22      + 14      + 13      + 48      + 54      + 21
```

3.
```
   66        41        17        34        88        72
 + 20      + 34      + 50      + 25      + 10      + 24
```

4.
```
   55        18        26        42        53        33
 + 31      + 51      + 51      + 32      + 41      +45
```

5.
```
   27        34        22        40        19        80
 + 21      + 25      + 76      + 39      + 50      + 19
```

6.
```
   43        26        35        34        55        48
 + 23      + 71      + 21      + 32      + 11      + 30
```

2-Digit Subtraction

Solve each problem.

Subtract the ones first.	36
6 minus 2 equals 4.	− 12
Then subtract the tens.	
3 minus 1 equals 2.	**24**

OK folks, let's hear it for 2-digit subtraction!

1.
$$86 - 32$$ $$52 - 12$$ $$67 - 45$$ $$95 - 30$$ $$87 - 26$$ $$48 - 33$$

2.
$$39 - 13$$ $$66 - 46$$ $$38 - 14$$ $$75 - 52$$ $$88 - 37$$ $$74 - 24$$

3.
$$47 - 15$$ $$96 - 73$$ $$58 - 54$$ $$81 - 21$$ $$57 - 33$$ $$49 - 25$$

4.
$$36 - 14$$ $$87 - 77$$ $$70 - 30$$ $$65 - 50$$ $$99 - 73$$ $$28 - 12$$

5.
$$97 - 25$$ $$64 - 23$$ $$72 - 22$$ $$89 - 55$$ $$55 - 14$$ $$83 - 20$$

6.
$$88 - 51$$ $$95 - 33$$ $$71 - 30$$ $$94 - 52$$ $$75 - 42$$ $$67 - 25$$

40

2-Digit Subtraction
Solve each problem.

> Be sure to subtract the ones first and then the tens!

1.	94	83	77	49	53	79
	− 12	− 22	− 21	− 27	− 32	− 54
	82					

2.	88	79	62	78	48	57
	− 31	− 58	− 40	− 32	− 17	− 33

3.	75	83	98	86	74	69
	− 24	− 11	− 37	− 45	− 34	− 12

4.	92	78	43	94	82	79
	− 80	− 47	− 32	− 12	− 51	− 34

5.	47	58	66	48	55	89
	− 25	− 36	− 23	− 32	− 21	− 37

6.	74	81	37	56	88	93
	− 32	− 61	− 15	− 43	− 34	− 71

2-Digit Addition with Regrouping

Solve each problem.

Don't forget to regroup if you need to.
Be sure to put the tens in the tens
column and add them with the other tens.

I
♥
regrouping!

1.
$$\begin{array}{r} \overset{1}{2}7 \\ + 24 \\ \hline 51 \end{array}$$
$$\begin{array}{r} 39 \\ + 53 \\ \hline \end{array}$$
$$\begin{array}{r} 46 \\ + 35 \\ \hline \end{array}$$
$$\begin{array}{r} 57 \\ + 29 \\ \hline \end{array}$$
$$\begin{array}{r} 49 \\ + 15 \\ \hline \end{array}$$
$$\begin{array}{r} 63 \\ + 27 \\ \hline \end{array}$$

2.
$$\begin{array}{r} 75 \\ + 19 \\ \hline \end{array}$$
$$\begin{array}{r} 93 \\ + 37 \\ \hline \end{array}$$
$$\begin{array}{r} 58 \\ + 34 \\ \hline \end{array}$$
$$\begin{array}{r} 64 \\ + 28 \\ \hline \end{array}$$
$$\begin{array}{r} 86 \\ + 17 \\ \hline \end{array}$$
$$\begin{array}{r} 47 \\ + 28 \\ \hline \end{array}$$

3.
$$\begin{array}{r} 66 \\ + 26 \\ \hline \end{array}$$
$$\begin{array}{r} 79 \\ + 32 \\ \hline \end{array}$$
$$\begin{array}{r} 43 \\ + 27 \\ \hline \end{array}$$
$$\begin{array}{r} 56 \\ + 58 \\ \hline \end{array}$$
$$\begin{array}{r} 98 \\ + 32 \\ \hline \end{array}$$
$$\begin{array}{r} 81 \\ + 59 \\ \hline \end{array}$$

4.
$$\begin{array}{r} 64 \\ + 17 \\ \hline \end{array}$$
$$\begin{array}{r} 57 \\ + 26 \\ \hline \end{array}$$
$$\begin{array}{r} 34 \\ + 49 \\ \hline \end{array}$$
$$\begin{array}{r} 25 \\ + 36 \\ \hline \end{array}$$
$$\begin{array}{r} 18 \\ + 28 \\ \hline \end{array}$$
$$\begin{array}{r} 27 \\ + 59 \\ \hline \end{array}$$

5.
$$\begin{array}{r} 43 \\ + 27 \\ \hline \end{array}$$
$$\begin{array}{r} 26 \\ + 36 \\ \hline \end{array}$$
$$\begin{array}{r} 27 \\ + 69 \\ \hline \end{array}$$
$$\begin{array}{r} 53 \\ + 37 \\ \hline \end{array}$$
$$\begin{array}{r} 33 \\ + 48 \\ \hline \end{array}$$
$$\begin{array}{r} 49 \\ + 27 \\ \hline \end{array}$$

6.
$$\begin{array}{r} 49 \\ + 25 \\ \hline \end{array}$$
$$\begin{array}{r} 35 \\ + 45 \\ \hline \end{array}$$
$$\begin{array}{r} 37 \\ + 38 \\ \hline \end{array}$$
$$\begin{array}{r} 89 \\ + 62 \\ \hline \end{array}$$
$$\begin{array}{r} 26 \\ + 68 \\ \hline \end{array}$$
$$\begin{array}{r} 38 \\ + 27 \\ \hline \end{array}$$

Math Connection—Grade 3—RBP3799   www.summerbridgeactivities.com   © RBP Books

2-Digit Addition with Regrouping

Solve each problem.

Remember to add the ones first!

1.	39 + 55	28 + 36	49 + 27	32 + 39	57 + 23	17 + 48
2.	47 + 27	68 + 29	71 + 19	28 + 48	37 + 28	48 + 32
3.	65 + 26	49 + 23	34 + 27	56 + 18	69 + 21	75 + 17
4.	45 + 28	29 + 56	49 + 24	41 + 19	33 + 68	69 + 22
5.	84 + 18	55 + 38	51 + 29	47 + 38	54 + 27	42 + 48
6.	59 + 17	44 + 28	37 + 54	82 + 19	73 + 18	93 + 27

2-Digit Subtraction with Regrouping

Solve each problem.

Subtract the ones. You can't subtract 7 from 2, so you'll have to regroup.

$$\begin{array}{r} 4\ 2 \\ -\ 2\ 7 \\ \hline \end{array}$$

To regroup, take 1 ten from 4 tens, leaving 3 tens. Add to the ones to make 12 ones. Now subtract. 12 − 7 = 5.

$$\begin{array}{r} {}^{3}\cancel{4}\ {}^{1}2 \\ -\ 2\ 7 \\ \hline 5 \end{array}$$

Subtract the tens. 3 tens minus 2 tens equals 1 ten.

$$\begin{array}{r} {}^{3}\cancel{4}\ {}^{1}2 \\ -\ 2\ 7 \\ \hline 1\ 5 \end{array}$$

1.

$$\begin{array}{r} 36 \\ -\ 17 \\ \hline \end{array} \qquad \begin{array}{r} 98 \\ -\ 19 \\ \hline \end{array} \qquad \begin{array}{r} 28 \\ -\ 9 \\ \hline \end{array} \qquad \begin{array}{r} 41 \\ -\ 15 \\ \hline \end{array} \qquad \begin{array}{r} 33 \\ -\ 17 \\ \hline \end{array} \qquad \begin{array}{r} 67 \\ -\ 18 \\ \hline \end{array}$$

2.

$$\begin{array}{r} 72 \\ -\ 53 \\ \hline \end{array} \qquad \begin{array}{r} 85 \\ -\ 27 \\ \hline \end{array} \qquad \begin{array}{r} 43 \\ -\ 29 \\ \hline \end{array} \qquad \begin{array}{r} 96 \\ -\ 37 \\ \hline \end{array} \qquad \begin{array}{r} 64 \\ -\ 36 \\ \hline \end{array} \qquad \begin{array}{r} 50 \\ -\ 18 \\ \hline \end{array}$$

3.

$$\begin{array}{r} 47 \\ -\ 19 \\ \hline \end{array} \qquad \begin{array}{r} 94 \\ -\ 26 \\ \hline \end{array} \qquad \begin{array}{r} 75 \\ -\ 39 \\ \hline \end{array} \qquad \begin{array}{r} 61 \\ -\ 22 \\ \hline \end{array} \qquad \begin{array}{r} 33 \\ -\ 19 \\ \hline \end{array} \qquad \begin{array}{r} 82 \\ -\ 35 \\ \hline \end{array}$$

4.

$$\begin{array}{r} 71 \\ -\ 46 \\ \hline \end{array} \qquad \begin{array}{r} 86 \\ -\ 47 \\ \hline \end{array} \qquad \begin{array}{r} 94 \\ -\ 35 \\ \hline \end{array} \qquad \begin{array}{r} 65 \\ -\ 27 \\ \hline \end{array} \qquad \begin{array}{r} 92 \\ -\ 44 \\ \hline \end{array} \qquad \begin{array}{r} 53 \\ -\ 29 \\ \hline \end{array}$$

5.

$$\begin{array}{r} 76 \\ -\ 38 \\ \hline \end{array} \qquad \begin{array}{r} 64 \\ -\ 35 \\ \hline \end{array} \qquad \begin{array}{r} 76 \\ -\ 27 \\ \hline \end{array} \qquad \begin{array}{r} 52 \\ -\ 44 \\ \hline \end{array} \qquad \begin{array}{r} 83 \\ -\ 25 \\ \hline \end{array} \qquad \begin{array}{r} 68 \\ -\ 49 \\ \hline \end{array}$$

6.

$$\begin{array}{r} 94 \\ -\ 25 \\ \hline \end{array} \qquad \begin{array}{r} 37 \\ -\ 19 \\ \hline \end{array} \qquad \begin{array}{r} 76 \\ -\ 29 \\ \hline \end{array} \qquad \begin{array}{r} 46 \\ -\ 18 \\ \hline \end{array} \qquad \begin{array}{r} 50 \\ -\ 14 \\ \hline \end{array} \qquad \begin{array}{r} 57 \\ -\ 29 \\ \hline \end{array}$$

2-Digit Subtraction with Regrouping

Solve each problem.

> Knowing your basic addition and subtraction facts makes even hard subtraction problems easy!

1.
   23   41   73   57   63   82
− 18 − 27 − 37 − 29 − 16 − 28

2.
   58   52   91   78   42   60
− 39 − 17 − 48 − 49 − 28 − 38

3.
   82   75   33   47   77   84
− 39 − 49 − 15 − 28 − 58 − 37

4.
   51   62   55   81   70   63
− 28 − 38 − 38 − 39 − 27 − 37

5.
   56   43   66   72   81   73
− 17 − 26 − 28 − 53 − 53 − 38

6.
   41   56   44   62   71   84
− 29 − 18 − 18 − 25 − 29 − 28

2-Digit Addition and Subtraction Practice

Solve each problem.

> Watch the signs!
> Regroup if you need to.

1.

$$87 - 29$$ $$29 + 37$$ $$51 - 23$$ $$26 + 45$$ $$35 + 57$$

2.

$$91 - 67$$ $$86 - 27$$ $$71 - 52$$ $$62 + 19$$ $$53 - 21$$

3.

$$47 + 13$$ $$84 + 58$$ $$31 - 19$$ $$93 - 36$$ $$44 + 48$$

4.

$$72 - 39$$ $$28 + 57$$ $$49 - 31$$ $$62 + 25$$ $$98 - 37$$

5.

$$88 - 49$$ $$29 + 18$$ $$77 - 58$$ $$66 + 26$$ $$11 + 78$$

6.

$$87 + 26$$ $$27 + 47$$ $$53 - 34$$ $$27 + 55$$ $$34 - 18$$

Math Connection—Grade 3—RBP3799   www.summerbridgeactivities.com   © RBP Books

2-Digit Addition and Subtraction Practice

Solve each problem.

Sometimes it's fun to use a calculator to check your answers.

1.	74 + 56	88 − 39	43 − 27	47 + 36	28 + 48
2.	82 − 47	51 + 19	84 + 17	35 − 18	67 − 29
3.	61 − 28	74 − 46	52 + 67	78 − 49	38 + 57
4.	43 + 59	73 + 18	81 − 28	38 + 24	62 − 44
5.	52 − 36	29 + 48	67 − 25	48 − 29	71 + 39
6.	73 − 57	18 + 37	27 + 56	70 − 37	81 − 26

www.summerbridgeactivities.com **Math Connection—Grade 3—RBP3799**

2-Digit Addition and Subtraction Problem Solving

Solve the problems. Do your work in the box. Write your answer on the line.

Dan has 24 dogs. 18 of his dogs are greyhounds. How many of his dogs are not greyhounds?

6 of the dogs are not greyhounds.

$$\begin{array}{r} 24 \\ -\ 18 \\ \hline \mathbf{6} \end{array}$$

This is a subtraction problem. I subtract the number of greyhounds from the total to find out how many of the dogs are not greyhounds.

1. Sam's basketball team scored 42 points. Nick's team only scored 28 points.

How many more points did Sam's team score than Nick's?

_____

2. Jan had 57 seashells.

Her aunt sent her 26 more seashells for her collection.

How many seashells does Jan have now?

_____

3. Nathan had 82 toy cars. He saved 15 special cars and gave the rest to his little cousins.

How many cars did he give to his cousins?

_____

4. A bike shop had 43 adult bikes and 38 children's bikes.

How many bikes did they have altogether?

_____

5. Alexis sold 35 boxes of cookies. Amanda sold 28 boxes.

How many more boxes of cookies did Alexis sell than Amanda?

_____

6. Phil had 34 books.

He lost 8 during his move.

How many books does he have left?

_____

Math Connection—Grade 3—RBP3799

www.summerbridgeactivities.com

© RBP Books

2-Digit Addition and Subtraction Problem Solving

Solve the problems. Do your work in the box. Write your answer on the line.

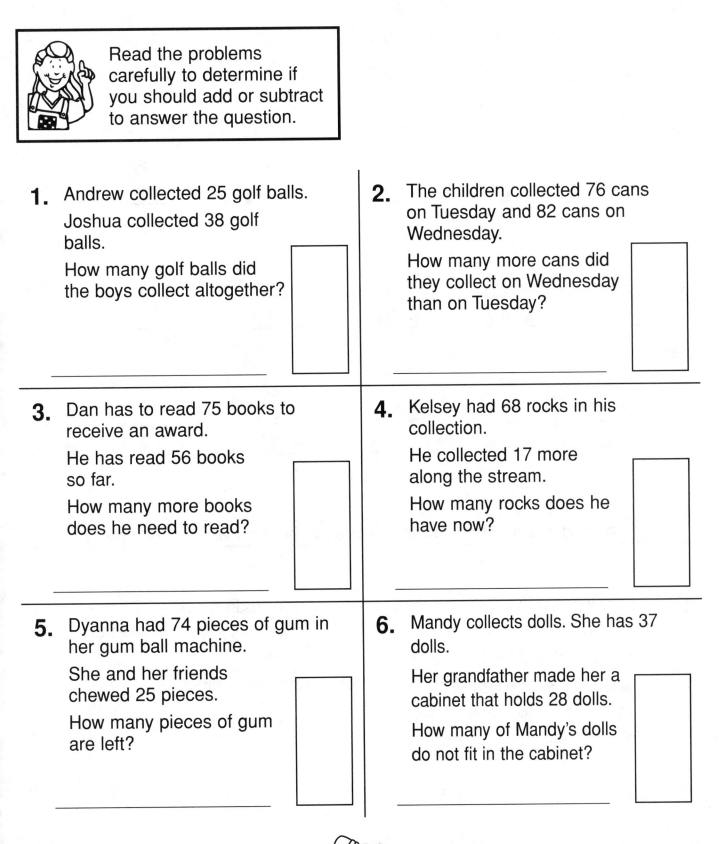

Read the problems carefully to determine if you should add or subtract to answer the question.

1. Andrew collected 25 golf balls.

Joshua collected 38 golf balls.

How many golf balls did the boys collect altogether?

_____

2. The children collected 76 cans on Tuesday and 82 cans on Wednesday.

How many more cans did they collect on Wednesday than on Tuesday?

_____

3. Dan has to read 75 books to receive an award.

He has read 56 books so far.

How many more books does he need to read?

_____

4. Kelsey had 68 rocks in his collection.

He collected 17 more along the stream.

How many rocks does he have now?

_____

5. Dyanna had 74 pieces of gum in her gum ball machine.

She and her friends chewed 25 pieces.

How many pieces of gum are left?

_____

6. Mandy collects dolls. She has 37 dolls.

Her grandfather made her a cabinet that holds 28 dolls.

How many of Mandy's dolls do not fit in the cabinet?

_____

2-Digit Addition and Subtraction Assessment

Solve the problems.

1.
45	56	27	83	34	25
+ 31	+ 21	+ 62	+ 16	+ 54	+ 40

2.
87	74	98	56	66	92
− 53	− 32	− 56	− 44	− 23	− 31

3.
64	75	49	83	72	58
+ 27	+ 48	+ 26	+ 29	+ 59	+ 37

4.
82	71	54	92	43	30
− 38	− 29	− 18	− 49	− 27	− 18

Solve the problem. Do your work in the box. Write your answer on the line.

5. Megan wanted to ride her bike 50 miles this month.

   She has ridden 37 miles.

   How many more miles does she need to ride to meet her goal?

   _____

6. Trevor rode his bike 27 miles on Saturday and 34 miles on Sunday.

   How many miles did he ride?

   _____

www.summerbridgeactivities.com

2-Digit Addition and Subtraction Assessment

Solve the problems.

1. $\begin{array}{r} 36 \\ +\ 22 \\ \hline \end{array}$ $\begin{array}{r} 48 \\ +\ 31 \\ \hline \end{array}$ $\begin{array}{r} 52 \\ +\ 37 \\ \hline \end{array}$ $\begin{array}{r} 71 \\ +\ 23 \\ \hline \end{array}$ $\begin{array}{r} 27 \\ +\ 41 \\ \hline \end{array}$ $\begin{array}{r} 63 \\ +\ 12 \\ \hline \end{array}$

2. $\begin{array}{r} 88 \\ -\ 43 \\ \hline \end{array}$ $\begin{array}{r} 79 \\ -\ 23 \\ \hline \end{array}$ $\begin{array}{r} 64 \\ -\ 31 \\ \hline \end{array}$ $\begin{array}{r} 97 \\ -\ 52 \\ \hline \end{array}$ $\begin{array}{r} 86 \\ -\ 30 \\ \hline \end{array}$ $\begin{array}{r} 75 \\ -\ 24 \\ \hline \end{array}$

3. $\begin{array}{r} 57 \\ +\ 34 \\ \hline \end{array}$ $\begin{array}{r} 66 \\ +\ 78 \\ \hline \end{array}$ $\begin{array}{r} 84 \\ +\ 26 \\ \hline \end{array}$ $\begin{array}{r} 39 \\ +\ 73 \\ \hline \end{array}$ $\begin{array}{r} 28 \\ +\ 33 \\ \hline \end{array}$ $\begin{array}{r} 46 \\ +\ 29 \\ \hline \end{array}$

4. $\begin{array}{r} 83 \\ -\ 28 \\ \hline \end{array}$ $\begin{array}{r} 78 \\ -\ 39 \\ \hline \end{array}$ $\begin{array}{r} 57 \\ -\ 19 \\ \hline \end{array}$ $\begin{array}{r} 72 \\ -\ 38 \\ \hline \end{array}$ $\begin{array}{r} 81 \\ -\ 14 \\ \hline \end{array}$ $\begin{array}{r} 93 \\ -\ 46 \\ \hline \end{array}$

Solve the problem. Do your work in the box. Write your answer on the line.

5. Mrs. Tripp's class read 82 books.

    Mrs. Tanner's class read 69 books.

    How many more books did Mrs. Tripp's class read?

    _____

6. Nick read 47 pages on Monday and 58 pages on Thursday.

    How many pages did he read in all?

    _____

51

3-Digit Addition
Solve each problem.

1. Add the ones.	2. Add the tens.	3. Add the hundreds.
4 6 2 + 1 3 4 ___6	4 6 2 + 1 3 4 __9 6	4 6 2 + 1 3 4 5 9 6

1.

182	231	825	436	325
+ 703	+ 547	+ 163	+ 562	+ 202

2.

274	641	908	365	207
+ 320	+ 345	+ 61	+ 424	+ 712

3.

352	475	724	650	298
+ 436	+ 510	+ 143	+ 227	+ 500

4.

525	631	447	319	752
+ 261	+ 155	+ 432	+ 450	+ 136

5.

933	547	830	626	487
+ 52	+ 131	+ 69	+ 331	+ 411

6.

631	488	562	723	506
+ 325	+ 211	+ 407	+ 166	+ 353

3-Digit Subtraction

Solve each problem.

1. Subtract the ones.   **2.** Subtract the tens.   **3.** Subtract the hundreds.

$$
\begin{array}{r}
5\ 6\ 4 \\
-\ 1\ 3\ 2 \\
\hline
2
\end{array}
\qquad
\begin{array}{r}
5\ 6\ 4 \\
-\ 1\ 3\ 2 \\
\hline
3\ 2
\end{array}
\qquad
\begin{array}{r}
5\ 6\ 4 \\
-\ 1\ 3\ 2 \\
\hline
4\ 3\ 2
\end{array}
$$

1.

684	634	835	738	325
− 253	− 421	− 610	− 502	− 102

2.

874	647	958	363	567
− 321	− 325	− 146	− 242	− 362

3.

283	488	695	719	894
− 220	− 351	− 233	− 305	− 752

4.

975	767	836	547	658
− 342	− 425	− 132	− 235	− 510

5.

393	649	786	999	887
− 173	− 235	− 526	− 683	− 346

3-Digit Addition with Regrouping

Solve each problem.

	1. Add the ones.	2. Add the tens.	3. Add the hundreds.
	Regroup 13 ones as 1 ten, 3 ones.	*Regroup 14 tens as 1 hundred, 4 tens.*	
	$3\ ^17\ 5$ $+\ 2\ 6\ 8$ 13	$^13\ ^17\ 5$ $+\ 2\ 6\ 8$ $14\ 3$	$^13\ 7\ 5$ $+\ 2\ 6\ 8$ $6\ 4\ 3$

1.

$$187 + 753$$ $$263 + 347$$ $$827 + 264$$ $$726 + 585$$ $$126 + 294$$

2.

$$283 + 328$$ $$268 + 345$$ $$418 + 199$$ $$385 + 826$$ $$297 + 765$$

3.

$$624 + 167$$ $$537 + 226$$ $$384 + 409$$ $$275 + 316$$ $$108 + 258$$

4.

$$843 + 127$$ $$426 + 236$$ $$527 + 169$$ $$753 + 237$$ $$633 + 148$$

5.

$$493 + 256$$ $$357 + 452$$ $$375 + 384$$ $$893 + 26$$ $$261 + 685$$

6.

$$540 + 387$$ $$385 + 250$$ $$255 + 493$$ $$649 + 271$$ $$477 + 333$$

Math Connection—Grade 3—RBP3799   www.summerbridgeactivities.com   © RBP Books

3-Digit Addition with Regrouping
Solve each problem.

Once you have adding 3-digit numbers down, you can add any number together. Just remember to always start with the ones and work your way through the columns to the left.

1.

$$283 + 168$$ $$497 + 205$$ $$176 + 640$$ $$325 + 867$$ $$651 + 179$$

2.

$$304 + 519$$ $$517 + 334$$ $$237 + 807$$ $$482 + 531$$ $$117 + 488$$

3.

$$624 + 276$$ $$431 + 382$$ $$329 + 682$$ $$772 + 405$$ $$532 + 489$$

4.

$$136 + 477$$ $$479 + 342$$ $$379 + 483$$ $$386 + 364$$ $$670 + 259$$

5.

$$823 + 357$$ $$937 + 468$$ $$736 + 136$$ $$648 + 246$$ $$462 + 369$$

6.

$$837 + 337$$ $$689 + 285$$ $$350 + 261$$ $$427 + 367$$ $$601 + 289$$

3-Digit Addition with Regrouping

Solve each problem.

Even adding big numbers is easy once you know your addition facts.

1.
$$276 + 157$$ $$382 + 490$$ $$293 + 504$$ $$337 + 285$$ $$561 + 249$$

2.
$$326 + 499$$ $$538 + 309$$ $$118 + 826$$ $$235 + 536$$ $$247 + 378$$

3.
$$518 + 392$$ $$298 + 212$$ $$327 + 467$$ $$538 + 217$$ $$491 + 388$$

4.
$$129 + 679$$ $$532 + 395$$ $$497 + 289$$ $$233 + 495$$ $$576 + 205$$

5.
$$803 + 258$$ $$967 + 168$$ $$436 + 636$$ $$628 + 181$$ $$330 + 289$$

6.
$$536 + 367$$ $$678 + 874$$ $$360 + 244$$ $$827 + 307$$ $$591 + 379$$

Math Connection—Grade 3—RBP3799   www.summerbridgeactivities.com

3-Digit Subtraction with Regrouping

Solve each problem.

	1. Start with the ones.	**2.** Look at the tens.	**3.** Subtract the hundreds.
	You can't take 6 from 4.	*You can't take 5 tens from 2 tens.*	

So borrow 1 ten from 3 tens, leaving 2 tens. Regroup 1 ten to make 14 ones. Then, subtract 14 − 6.

$$5 \; {}^2\!\!\not{3} \; {}^1\!4$$
$$- \; 2 \; 5 \; | \; 6$$
$$\overline{ 8}$$

So borrow 1 hundred from 5 hundreds, leaving 4 hundreds. Regroup to make 12 tens. Then, subtract 12 − 5.

$${}^4\!\not{5} \; {}^{12}\!\!\not{3} \; {}^1\!4$$
$$- \; 2 \; 5 \; 6$$
$$\overline{ 7 \; 8}$$

$${}^4\!\not{5} \; 3 \; 4$$
$$- \; 2 \; 5 \; 6$$
$$\overline{2 \; 7 \; 8}$$

1.
$$\begin{array}{r} 837 \\ -138 \\ \hline \end{array} \quad \begin{array}{r} 516 \\ -247 \\ \hline \end{array} \quad \begin{array}{r} 825 \\ -356 \\ \hline \end{array} \quad \begin{array}{r} 713 \\ -284 \\ \hline \end{array} \quad \begin{array}{r} 624 \\ -367 \\ \hline \end{array}$$

2.
$$\begin{array}{r} 283 \\ -96 \\ \hline \end{array} \quad \begin{array}{r} 567 \\ -275 \\ \hline \end{array} \quad \begin{array}{r} 928 \\ -189 \\ \hline \end{array} \quad \begin{array}{r} 785 \\ -496 \\ \hline \end{array} \quad \begin{array}{r} 497 \\ -269 \\ \hline \end{array}$$

3.
$$\begin{array}{r} 553 \\ -129 \\ \hline \end{array} \quad \begin{array}{r} 476 \\ -138 \\ \hline \end{array} \quad \begin{array}{r} 764 \\ -335 \\ \hline \end{array} \quad \begin{array}{r} 676 \\ -227 \\ \hline \end{array} \quad \begin{array}{r} 952 \\ -344 \\ \hline \end{array}$$

4.
$$\begin{array}{r} 837 \\ -253 \\ \hline \end{array} \quad \begin{array}{r} 689 \\ -496 \\ \hline \end{array} \quad \begin{array}{r} 941 \\ -250 \\ \hline \end{array} \quad \begin{array}{r} 277 \\ -193 \\ \hline \end{array} \quad \begin{array}{r} 765 \\ -295 \\ \hline \end{array}$$

5.
$$\begin{array}{r} 463 \\ -182 \\ \hline \end{array} \quad \begin{array}{r} 570 \\ -143 \\ \hline \end{array} \quad \begin{array}{r} 857 \\ -329 \\ \hline \end{array} \quad \begin{array}{r} 986 \\ -595 \\ \hline \end{array} \quad \begin{array}{r} 662 \\ -456 \\ \hline \end{array}$$

www.summerbridgeactivities.com   Math Connection—Grade 3—RBP3799

3-Digit Subtraction with Regrouping

Solve each problem.

Just like addition, start with the ones and work your way through the columns to the left. Subtracting big numbers is easy once you get the hang of it!

1.
$$\begin{array}{r} 373 \\ -149 \\ \hline \end{array}$$
$$\begin{array}{r} 484 \\ -185 \\ \hline \end{array}$$
$$\begin{array}{r} 976 \\ -689 \\ \hline \end{array}$$
$$\begin{array}{r} 317 \\ -\ 89 \\ \hline \end{array}$$
$$\begin{array}{r} 621 \\ -166 \\ \hline \end{array}$$

2.
$$\begin{array}{r} 602 \\ -219 \\ \hline \end{array}$$
$$\begin{array}{r} 407 \\ -138 \\ \hline \end{array}$$
$$\begin{array}{r} 887 \\ -309 \\ \hline \end{array}$$
$$\begin{array}{r} 431 \\ -161 \\ \hline \end{array}$$
$$\begin{array}{r} 817 \\ -468 \\ \hline \end{array}$$

3.
$$\begin{array}{r} 621 \\ -286 \\ \hline \end{array}$$
$$\begin{array}{r} 444 \\ -297 \\ \hline \end{array}$$
$$\begin{array}{r} 309 \\ -168 \\ \hline \end{array}$$
$$\begin{array}{r} 782 \\ -339 \\ \hline \end{array}$$
$$\begin{array}{r} 501 \\ -289 \\ \hline \end{array}$$

4.
$$\begin{array}{r} 842 \\ -377 \\ \hline \end{array}$$
$$\begin{array}{r} 578 \\ -349 \\ \hline \end{array}$$
$$\begin{array}{r} 958 \\ -483 \\ \hline \end{array}$$
$$\begin{array}{r} 586 \\ -398 \\ \hline \end{array}$$
$$\begin{array}{r} 680 \\ -269 \\ \hline \end{array}$$

5.
$$\begin{array}{r} 831 \\ -397 \\ \hline \end{array}$$
$$\begin{array}{r} 927 \\ -458 \\ \hline \end{array}$$
$$\begin{array}{r} 746 \\ -188 \\ \hline \end{array}$$
$$\begin{array}{r} 845 \\ -276 \\ \hline \end{array}$$
$$\begin{array}{r} 452 \\ -179 \\ \hline \end{array}$$

6.
$$\begin{array}{r} 829 \\ -238 \\ \hline \end{array}$$
$$\begin{array}{r} 582 \\ -185 \\ \hline \end{array}$$
$$\begin{array}{r} 351 \\ -169 \\ \hline \end{array}$$
$$\begin{array}{r} 427 \\ -\ 68 \\ \hline \end{array}$$
$$\begin{array}{r} 501 \\ -389 \\ \hline \end{array}$$

3-Digit Subtraction with Regrouping

Solve each problem.

> Keep memorizing your facts if you're still having to use your fingers!

1.	873 − 267	454 − 275	672 − 348	305 − 107	681 − 269
2.	244 − 79	503 − 134	732 − 207	402 − 167	715 − 368
3.	604 − 177	731 − 292	929 − 678	672 − 206	541 − 389
4.	726 − 437	870 − 382	579 − 383	781 − 394	573 − 149
5.	804 − 367	922 − 369	746 − 158	612 − 286	432 − 116
6.	823 − 387	680 − 293	953 − 265	411 − 143	681 − 299

3-Digit Addition and Subtraction Practice
Solve each problem.

Watch the signs. Mixed addition and subtraction practice can be tricky.

1.
$$187 + 838$$ $$492 - 185$$ $$886 + 340$$ $$725 + 287$$ $$630 - 168$$

2.
$$317 + 415$$ $$617 + 304$$ $$227 - 109$$ $$380 + 739$$ $$817 - 468$$

3.
$$374 - 176$$ $$537 + 285$$ $$620 - 182$$ $$972 + 409$$ $$732 - 269$$

4.
$$236 + 587$$ $$279 + 373$$ $$660 - 153$$ $$456 + 464$$ $$770 - 262$$

5.
$$803 - 377$$ $$917 - 458$$ $$746 + 336$$ $$548 + 476$$ $$476 + 389$$

6.
$$847 + 387$$ $$689 - 295$$ $$550 + 281$$ $$627 + 277$$ $$649 + 279$$

3-Digit Addition and Subtraction Practice

Start from the center and work outward to answer each problem.

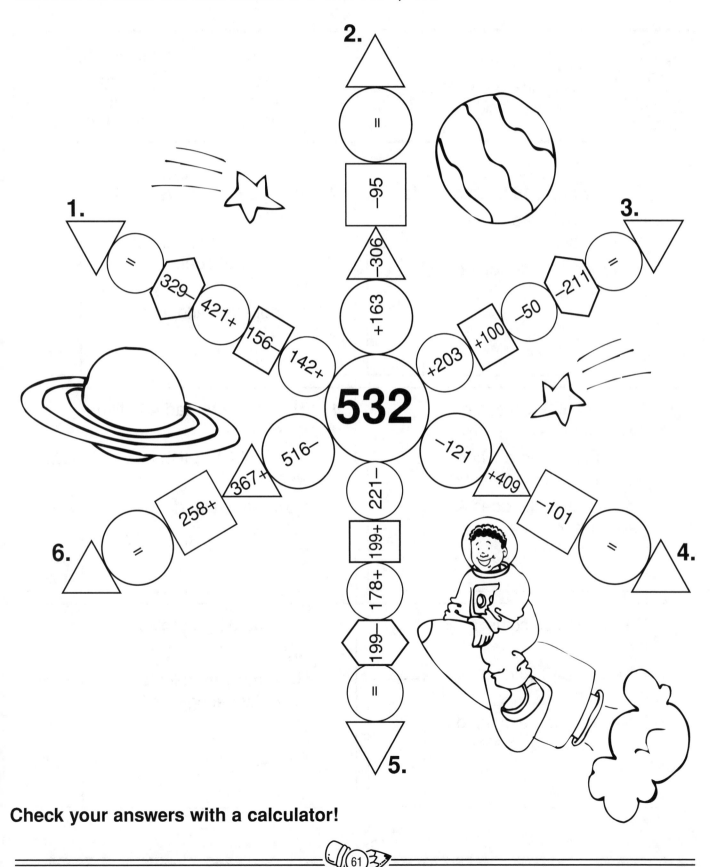

Check your answers with a calculator!

www.summerbridgeactivities.com Math Connection—Grade 3—RBP3799

3-Digit Addition and Subtraction Problem Solving

Solve the problems. Do your work in the box. Write your answer on the line.

	Key Words for Problem Solving	
Add or subtract? Look for these key words to help you decide.	**Add** in all altogether	**Subtract** left more than

1. Roberto had 346 trading cards.

He sold 188 cards at a trading card show.

How many cards does he have left?

_____

2. Mindy's class saved 121 soup labels.

The rest of the school saved 699 labels.

How many labels does the school have altogether?

_____

3. Alex had 623 rocks in his collection.

He found 17 more when he went hiking last weekend.

How many rocks does Alex have in all?

_____

4. The pet store had 435 fish for sale.

They sold 178 fish last week.

How many fish do they have left?

_____

5. Devin has 728 coins in his collection.

Kate has 649 coins in her collection.

How many more coins does Devin have than Kate?

_____

6. Kim has 321 marbles.

Kris has 399 marbles.

How many marbles do they have altogether?

_____

Math Connection—Grade 3—RBP3799   www.summerbridgeactivities.com   © RBP Books

3-Digit Addition and Subtraction Problem Solving

Solve the problems. Do your work in the box. Write your answer on the line.

Read the problems carefully. Look for the key words to help you know whether to add or subtract to find the answer.

1. Anthony had 348 pennies.

His brother had 239.

How many more pennies did Anthony have than his brother?

_____

2. Celeste collected 479 aluminum cans.

Nicole collected 742 cans.

How many cans did the girls collect altogether?

_____

3. The electronics store had 371 televisions in stock.

They sold 138 on the weekend.

How many televisions do they have left?

_____

4. My big brother Matt weighs 189 pounds.

His friend weighs 202 pounds.

How much less does Matt weigh than his friend?

_____

5. The school library has 879 non-fiction books and 932 fiction books.

How many books does the library have altogether?

_____

6. The girls earned 487 points for selling cookies.

The boys earned 399 points.

How many more points did the girls earn than the boys?

_____

3-Digit Addition and Subtraction Assessment

Solve the problems.

1.
$$732 + 211$$
$$342 + 153$$
$$621 + 148$$
$$322 + 361$$
$$851 + 47$$

2.
$$866 - 312$$
$$739 - 417$$
$$986 - 352$$
$$869 - 356$$
$$479 - 153$$

3.
$$783 + 348$$
$$479 + 188$$
$$782 + 718$$
$$835 + 386$$
$$589 + 347$$

4.
$$632 - 278$$
$$841 - 147$$
$$775 - 289$$
$$624 - 346$$
$$540 - 183$$

Solve the problem. Do your work in the box. Write your answer on the line.

5. Braxton scored 478 points on the computer game.

Nick scored 661 points.

How many more points did Nick score than Braxton?

_____

6. Jana has collected 322 bottle caps.

Her brother has collected 489 bottle caps.

How many caps do they have altogether?

_____

3-Digit Addition and Subtraction Assessment

Solve the problems.

1.
834	732	653	610	566
+ 121	+ 214	+ 243	+ 239	+ 123

2.
442	883	749	686	545
− 120	− 451	− 327	− 355	− 302

3.
871	578	889	746	608
+ 249	+ 245	+ 122	+ 358	+ 376

4.
882	675	551	482	912
− 389	− 247	− 298	− 195	− 487

Solve the problem. Do your work in the box. Write your answer on the line.

5. There are 489 third grade students in one class and 492 in the other class.

   How many third graders are there altogether?

   _____

6. There are 987 kindergartners and 899 first grade students.

   How many more kindergartners are there than first graders?

   _____

4-Digit Addition

Solve each problem.

Add the ones first, then the tens, then the hundreds, and finally, the thousands.
Regroup if you need to.

I'm sure you'll have no problem finishing these problems!

1.
$$\begin{array}{r}\overset{1\ 1}{3{,}261} \\ +\ 5{,}239 \\ \hline \mathbf{8{,}500}\end{array}$$
$$\begin{array}{r}4{,}639 \\ +\ 2{,}073 \\ \hline\end{array}$$
$$\begin{array}{r}7{,}216 \\ +\ 2{,}593 \\ \hline\end{array}$$
$$\begin{array}{r}5{,}952 \\ +\ 3{,}128 \\ \hline\end{array}$$
$$\begin{array}{r}1{,}794 \\ +\ 2{,}607 \\ \hline\end{array}$$

2.
$$\begin{array}{r}2{,}773 \\ +\ 3{,}535 \\ \hline\end{array}$$
$$\begin{array}{r}9{,}076 \\ +\ 3{,}970 \\ \hline\end{array}$$
$$\begin{array}{r}6{,}415 \\ +\ 1{,}765 \\ \hline\end{array}$$
$$\begin{array}{r}4{,}701 \\ +\ 6{,}354 \\ \hline\end{array}$$
$$\begin{array}{r}8{,}213 \\ +\ 1{,}529 \\ \hline\end{array}$$

3.
$$\begin{array}{r}3{,}257 \\ +\ 4{,}809 \\ \hline\end{array}$$
$$\begin{array}{r}9{,}935 \\ +\ 1{,}260 \\ \hline\end{array}$$
$$\begin{array}{r}1{,}224 \\ +\ 8{,}967 \\ \hline\end{array}$$
$$\begin{array}{r}6{,}597 \\ +\ 3{,}212 \\ \hline\end{array}$$
$$\begin{array}{r}4{,}165 \\ +\ 7{,}042 \\ \hline\end{array}$$

4.
$$\begin{array}{r}7{,}309 \\ +\ 4{,}597 \\ \hline\end{array}$$
$$\begin{array}{r}3{,}295 \\ +\ 4{,}305 \\ \hline\end{array}$$
$$\begin{array}{r}5{,}716 \\ +\ 1{,}708 \\ \hline\end{array}$$
$$\begin{array}{r}6{,}907 \\ +\ 4{,}132 \\ \hline\end{array}$$
$$\begin{array}{r}8{,}813 \\ +\ 2{,}076 \\ \hline\end{array}$$

5.
$$\begin{array}{r}1{,}943 \\ +\ 3{,}065 \\ \hline\end{array}$$
$$\begin{array}{r}2{,}967 \\ +\ 7{,}120 \\ \hline\end{array}$$
$$\begin{array}{r}3{,}846 \\ +\ 2{,}195 \\ \hline\end{array}$$
$$\begin{array}{r}6{,}381 \\ +\ 5{,}436 \\ \hline\end{array}$$
$$\begin{array}{r}5{,}490 \\ +\ 6{,}327 \\ \hline\end{array}$$

6.
$$\begin{array}{r}8{,}361 \\ +\ 4{,}209 \\ \hline\end{array}$$
$$\begin{array}{r}5{,}639 \\ +\ 2{,}076 \\ \hline\end{array}$$
$$\begin{array}{r}1{,}735 \\ +\ 3{,}291 \\ \hline\end{array}$$
$$\begin{array}{r}2{,}465 \\ +\ 3{,}637 \\ \hline\end{array}$$
$$\begin{array}{r}9{,}675 \\ +\ 2{,}404 \\ \hline\end{array}$$

Math Connection—Grade 3—RBP3799   www.summerbridgeactivities.com   © RBP Books

4-Digit Subtraction

Solve each problem.

> Take one column at a time.
> Start with the ones.
> Regroup if you need to.

I love math this much!

1.
$$\begin{array}{r} \overset{8}{9},\overset{\overset{1}{3}}{7}\overset{\overset{6}{ }}{\overset{\overset{1}{ }}{5}} \\ -\ 4,969 \\ \hline \mathbf{4,406} \end{array}$$

$$\begin{array}{r} 2,772 \\ -\ 1,476 \\ \hline \end{array}$$

$$\begin{array}{r} 3,943 \\ -\ 1,876 \\ \hline \end{array}$$

$$\begin{array}{r} 5,814 \\ -\ 2,867 \\ \hline \end{array}$$

$$\begin{array}{r} 5,932 \\ -\ 3,845 \\ \hline \end{array}$$

2.
$$\begin{array}{r} 7,403 \\ -\ 2,675 \\ \hline \end{array}$$

$$\begin{array}{r} 9,800 \\ -\ 3,765 \\ \hline \end{array}$$

$$\begin{array}{r} 5,639 \\ -\ 1,879 \\ \hline \end{array}$$

$$\begin{array}{r} 7,860 \\ -\ 1,895 \\ \hline \end{array}$$

$$\begin{array}{r} 6,657 \\ -\ 5,575 \\ \hline \end{array}$$

3.
$$\begin{array}{r} 8,207 \\ -\ 4,648 \\ \hline \end{array}$$

$$\begin{array}{r} 9,730 \\ -\ 4,698 \\ \hline \end{array}$$

$$\begin{array}{r} 7,796 \\ -\ 2,994 \\ \hline \end{array}$$

$$\begin{array}{r} 3,905 \\ -\ 1,847 \\ \hline \end{array}$$

$$\begin{array}{r} 5,667 \\ -\ 2,909 \\ \hline \end{array}$$

4.
$$\begin{array}{r} 8,436 \\ -\ 7,527 \\ \hline \end{array}$$

$$\begin{array}{r} 6,943 \\ -\ 2,880 \\ \hline \end{array}$$

$$\begin{array}{r} 3,845 \\ -\ 1,966 \\ \hline \end{array}$$

$$\begin{array}{r} 8,560 \\ -\ 2,483 \\ \hline \end{array}$$

$$\begin{array}{r} 9,454 \\ -\ 2,087 \\ \hline \end{array}$$

5.
$$\begin{array}{r} 7,571 \\ -\ 3,875 \\ \hline \end{array}$$

$$\begin{array}{r} 5,965 \\ -\ 1,879 \\ \hline \end{array}$$

$$\begin{array}{r} 4,739 \\ -\ 3,465 \\ \hline \end{array}$$

$$\begin{array}{r} 7,430 \\ -\ 2,767 \\ \hline \end{array}$$

$$\begin{array}{r} 8,956 \\ -\ 3,979 \\ \hline \end{array}$$

www.summerbridgeactivities.com

Math Connection—Grade 3—RBP3799

4-Digit Addition and Subtraction Practice

Solve each problem.

> Watch the signs!
> Regroup if you need to.

You can do it!

1. $\begin{array}{r} 7,345 \\ + 2,762 \\ \hline \end{array}$ $\begin{array}{r} 3,210 \\ - 1,809 \\ \hline \end{array}$ $\begin{array}{r} 8,457 \\ - 4,312 \\ \hline \end{array}$ $\begin{array}{r} 4,091 \\ + 2,139 \\ \hline \end{array}$

2. $\begin{array}{r} 8,105 \\ - 4,560 \\ \hline \end{array}$ $\begin{array}{r} 1,719 \\ + 1,896 \\ \hline \end{array}$ $\begin{array}{r} 4,368 \\ - 1,492 \\ \hline \end{array}$ $\begin{array}{r} 8,121 \\ - 2,738 \\ \hline \end{array}$

3. $\begin{array}{r} 5,361 \\ + 1,762 \\ \hline \end{array}$ $\begin{array}{r} 3,800 \\ - 1,279 \\ \hline \end{array}$ $\begin{array}{r} 3,436 \\ + 5,371 \\ \hline \end{array}$ $\begin{array}{r} 4,487 \\ + 2,234 \\ \hline \end{array}$

4. $\begin{array}{r} 7,820 \\ - 3,458 \\ \hline \end{array}$ $\begin{array}{r} 6,941 \\ + 1,354 \\ \hline \end{array}$ $\begin{array}{r} 3,694 \\ + 2,208 \\ \hline \end{array}$ $\begin{array}{r} 5,784 \\ - 2,893 \\ \hline \end{array}$

5. $\begin{array}{r} 7,147 \\ + 1,522 \\ \hline \end{array}$ $\begin{array}{r} 7,004 \\ - 1,779 \\ \hline \end{array}$ $\begin{array}{r} 8,247 \\ - 3,544 \\ \hline \end{array}$ $\begin{array}{r} 5,906 \\ + 2,087 \\ \hline \end{array}$

Math Connection—Grade 3—RBP3799   www.summerbridgeactivities.com   © RBP Books

4-Digit Addition and Subtraction Problem Solving

Solve the problems. Do your work in the box. Write your answer on the line.

1.

2,479 people went to the concert on Friday night.
3,210 people went to the concert on Saturday night.

a. How many people went to the concert?

_____

b. How many more people attended on Saturday night than Friday night?

_____

2.

1,324 students graduated from East High School.
1,129 students graduated from West High School.

a. How many students graduated from the two high schools?

_____

b. How many more students graduated from East High than West High?

_____

3.

8,721 people live in Littletown.
7,820 people live in Smalltown.

a. How many more people live in Littletown than in Smalltown?

_____

b. How many people live in the two towns?

_____

Measuring with Inches and Feet

Complete each sentence. Choose the measurement that makes the most sense.

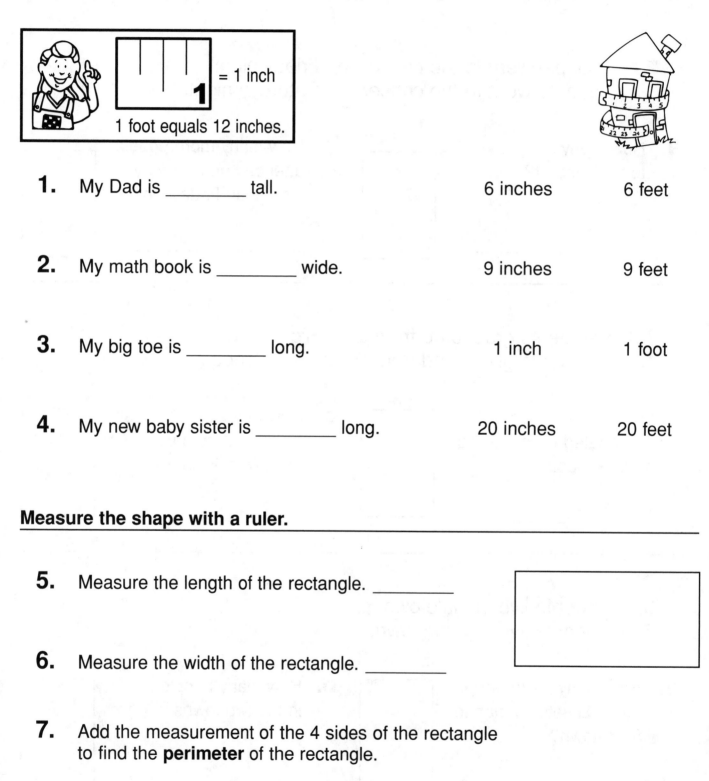

1. My Dad is _____ tall.   6 inches   6 feet

2. My math book is _____ wide.   9 inches   9 feet

3. My big toe is _____ long.   1 inch   1 foot

4. My new baby sister is _____ long. 20 inches   20 feet

Measure the shape with a ruler.

5. Measure the length of the rectangle. _____

6. Measure the width of the rectangle. _____

7. Add the measurement of the 4 sides of the rectangle
to find the **perimeter** of the rectangle.

_____ + _____ + _____ + _____ = _____

Measuring with Centimeters
Use a centimeter ruler to measure.

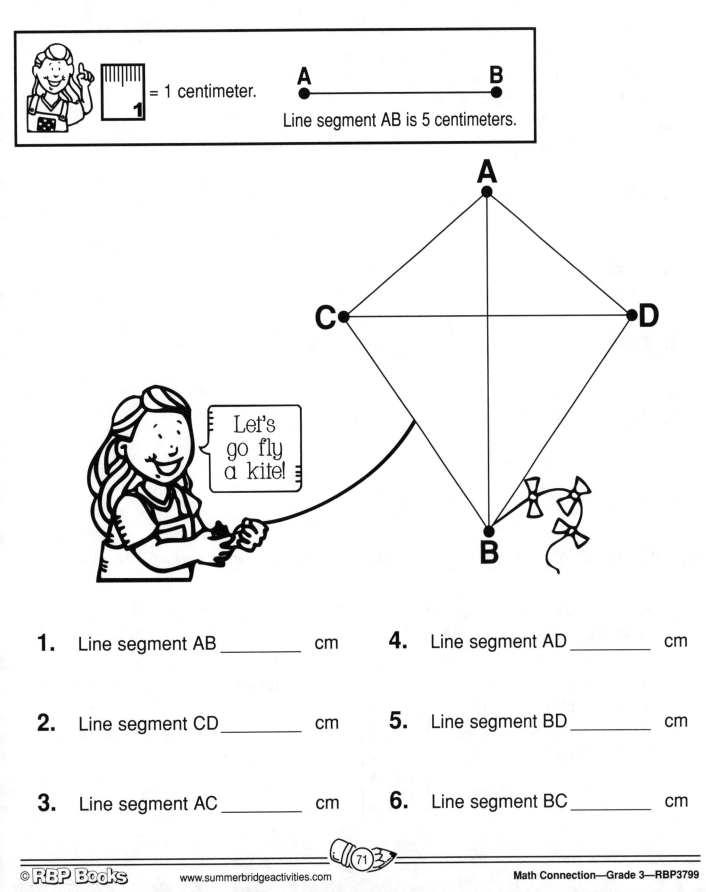

| | = 1 centimeter. | Line segment AB is 5 centimeters. |

1. Line segment AB _____ cm   **4.** Line segment AD _____ cm

2. Line segment CD _____ cm   **5.** Line segment BD _____ cm

3. Line segment AC _____ cm   **6.** Line segment BC _____ cm

Problem Solving with Measurement

Use >, <, or = to make each problem correct.

 Inches and feet are called **standard** measurements. Centimeters and meters are called **metric** measurements.

1. 1 foot   ◯   10 inches

2. 1 inch   ◯   1 centimeter

3. 1 foot   ◯   12 inches

4. 22 inches   ◯   2 feet

5. 3 centimeters   ◯   1 inch

Solve the problem. Do your work in the box. Write your answer on the line.

6. Kaedyn has a piece of string that is 45 inches long. She needs 13 inches of string to make a necklace. How many inches of string will she have left after she makes her necklace?

_____

7. Michael had a stick that was 15 inches long. He needed a stick that was 1 foot. How much did Michael need to cut from the stick?

_____

Math Connection—Grade 3—RBP3799   www.summerbridgeactivities.com   © RBP Books

Telling Time: Writing Time

Write the time shown on these clocks.

> Remember, the short hand is the hour hand, and the long hand is the minute hand.

Time to write time!

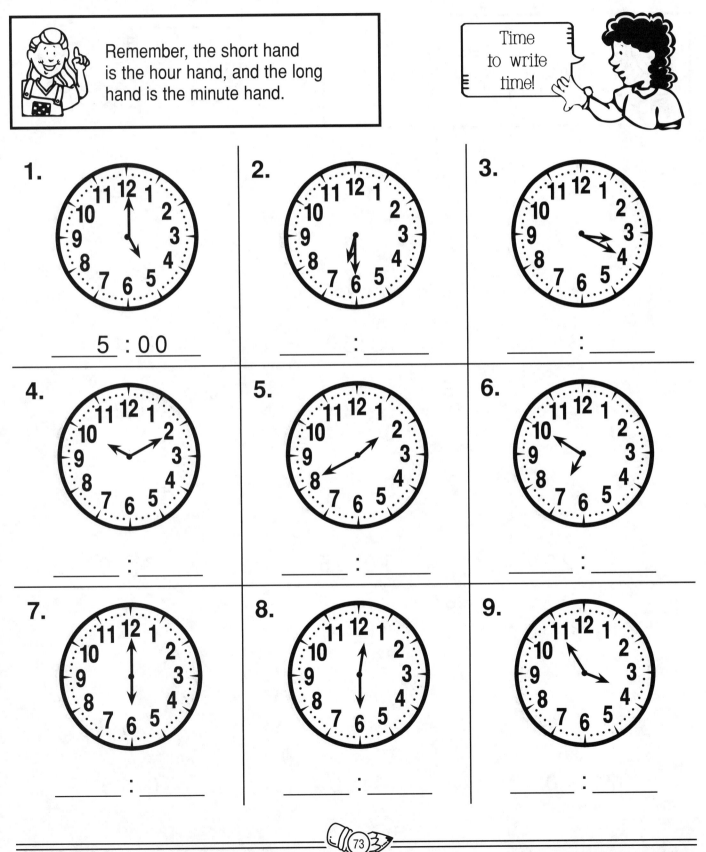

1.   5 : 00

2.   ___ : ___

3.   ___ : ___

4.   ___ : ___

5.   ___ : ___

6.   ___ : ___

7.   ___ : ___

8.   ___ : ___

9.   ___ : ___

Telling Time: Drawing Clock Hands

Draw the hands on the clocks to show the time.

Draw the hour hand first.
Then count by 5s to draw the
minute hand.

Time to
draw clock
hands!

1. 8:35

2. 9:50

3. 6:45

4. 12:20

5. 10:25

6. 7:50

7. 11:10

8. 4:40

9. 6:15

Math Connection—Grade 3—RBP3799   www.summerbridgeactivities.com   © RBP Books

Telling Time: Practice

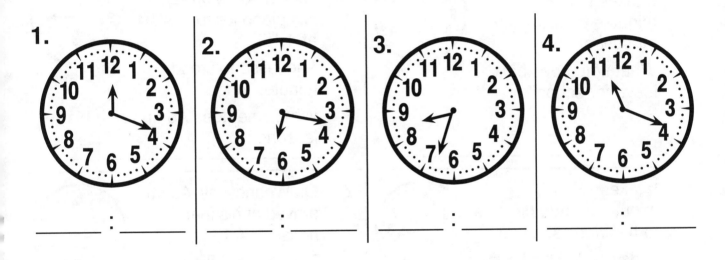

There are 5 minutes between each number on a clock.

We read the time on this clock as nine seventeen. We write the time as 9:17.

Write the time shown on each clock.

1.

2.

3.

4.

_____ : _____

_____ : _____

_____ : _____

_____ : _____

Draw hands to show the time on each clock.

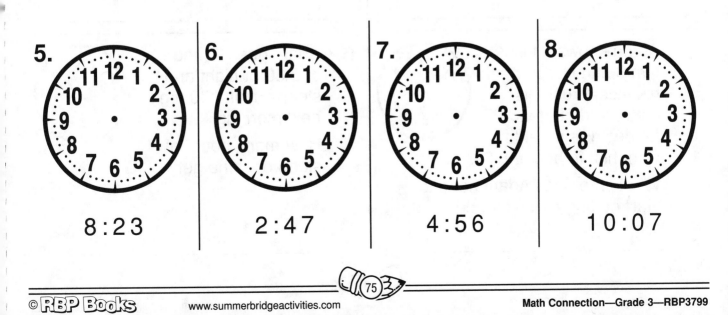

5.

6.

7.

8.

8 : 23

2 : 47

4 : 56

10 : 07

www.summerbridgeactivities.com

Math Connection—Grade 3—RBP3799

Telling Time: Problem Solving

Answer the questions.

 Use the clocks to help you answer the questions. Start with the time given and count forward or backward, depending on the question.

 What time is it when an elephant sits on your watch?

 Time to get a new watch!

1. Adam gets up at 7:30.

It takes him 25 minutes to get ready for school.

What time does he leave for school?

_____

2. Adam has piano lessons on Monday. His piano lessons start at 4:15.

The lessons are 25 minutes long.

What time does Adam finish his lessons?

_____

3. It takes Adam 7 minutes to ride his bike to his friend's house.

Today he left his house at 3:17.

What time will he get to his friend's house?

_____

4. On Wednesday, Adam arrived at his friend's house at 4:13.

They played for 1 hour and 30 minutes.

What time did Adam go home?

_____

5. Adam knows it takes him 9 minutes to wash his face, brush his teeth, and get ready for bed. His parents want him in bed at 8:30.

What time does Adam need to start getting ready for bed?

_____

6. Adam goes to bed at 8:30 at night and sleeps until 7:30 the next morning.

How many hours of sleep does he get?

_____

Telling Time: Problem Solving

Answer the questions.

Remember, **A.M.** refers to the morning time from 12:00 midnight until 12:00 noon. **P.M.** refers to the time from after 12:00 noon until 12:00 midnight.

1. Isabella wants to watch a show at 8:00 p.m.

It is 7:23 p.m.

How many more minutes before the show starts?

2. Cade's favorite show starts at 7:30 p.m.

It is 90 minutes long.

What time will the show end?

3. Taylor's favorite show starts at 4:30 p.m.

It is 30 minutes long.

It is 4:53 p.m.

How many more minutes until the show ends?

4. Melissa watched a movie that started at 7:00 p.m.

It lasted 1 hour and 47 minutes.

What time did the movie end?

5. Jonathan started watching a show at 4:16 p.m.

He turned the television off at 5:37 p.m.

How long did he watch television?

6. Chelsea watched two 30-minute shows on Monday, one 30-minute show on Wednesday, and three 30-minute shows on Friday.

How many hours of television did she watch that week?

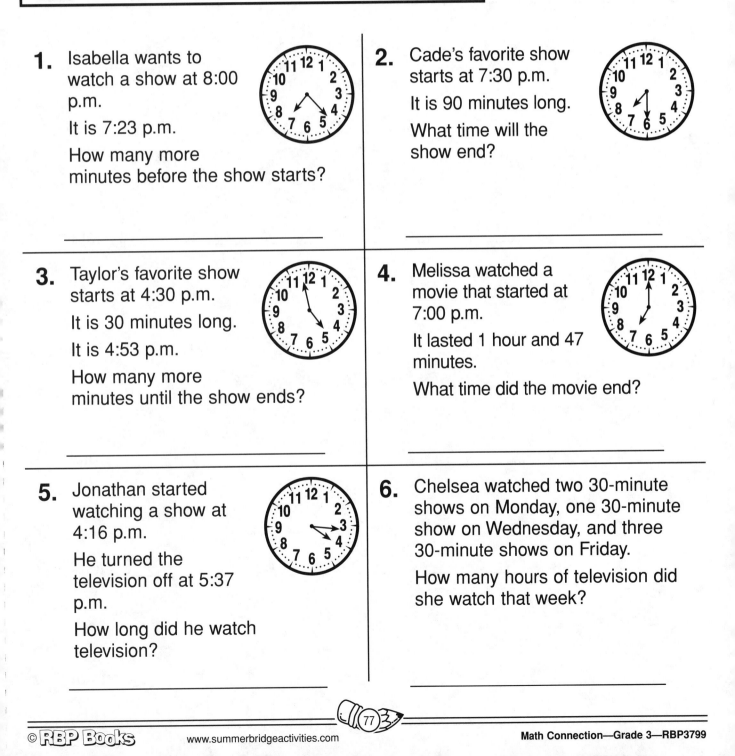

Counting Coins

Practice skip-counting pennies, nickels, dimes, quarters, and half-dollars.

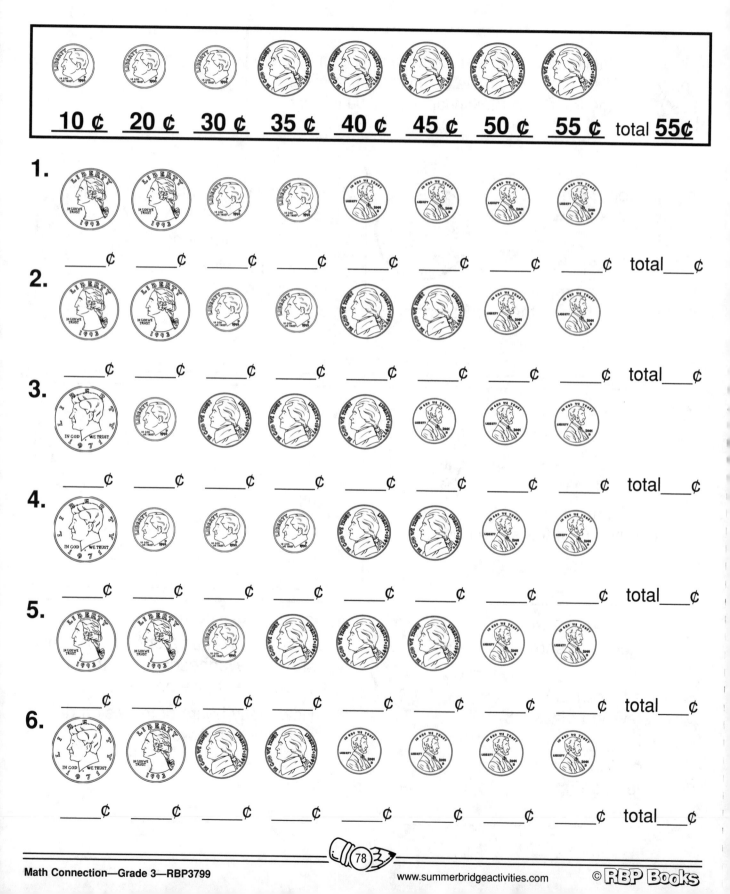

<u>10</u> ¢   <u>20</u> ¢   <u>30</u> ¢   <u>35</u> ¢   <u>40</u> ¢   <u>45</u> ¢   <u>50</u> ¢   <u>55</u> ¢   total <u>55¢</u>

1.

____ ¢   ____ ¢   ____ ¢   ____ ¢   ____ ¢   ____ ¢   ____ ¢   ____ ¢   total ____ ¢

2.

____ ¢   ____ ¢   ____ ¢   ____ ¢   ____ ¢   ____ ¢   ____ ¢   ____ ¢   total ____ ¢

3.

____ ¢   ____ ¢   ____ ¢   ____ ¢   ____ ¢   ____ ¢   ____ ¢   ____ ¢   total ____ ¢

4.

____ ¢   ____ ¢   ____ ¢   ____ ¢   ____ ¢   ____ ¢   ____ ¢   ____ ¢   total ____ ¢

5.

____ ¢   ____ ¢   ____ ¢   ____ ¢   ____ ¢   ____ ¢   ____ ¢   ____ ¢   total ____ ¢

6.

____ ¢   ____ ¢   ____ ¢   ____ ¢   ____ ¢   ____ ¢   ____ ¢   ____ ¢   total ____ ¢

Counting Coins

Count the coins. Write the total.

Write the total amount of the coins. Count the coins with the highest value first.

I'm saving my money for a new basketball hoop!

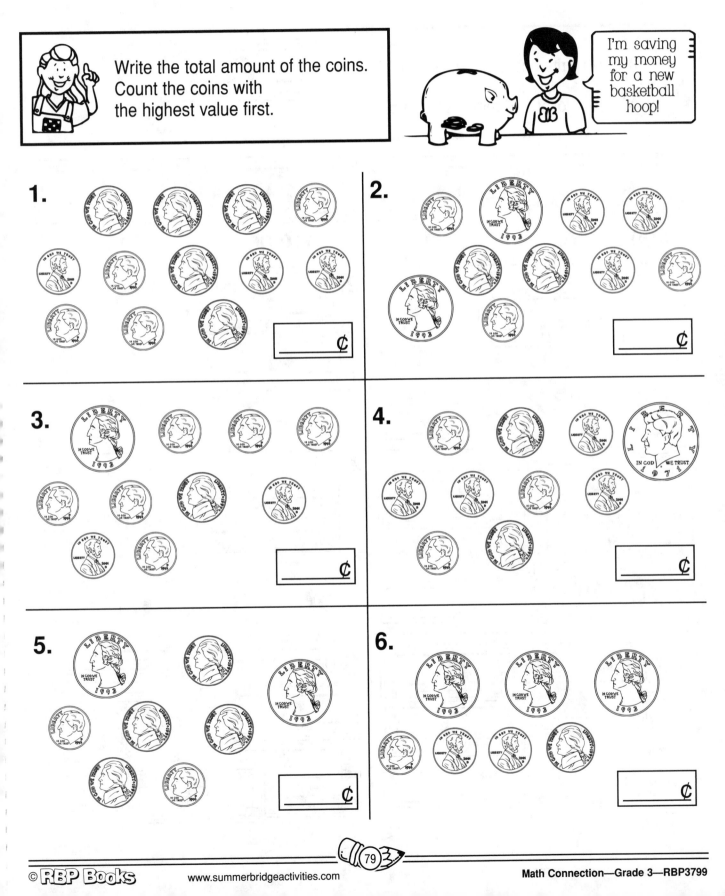

1. _____ ¢

2. _____ ¢

3. _____ ¢

4. _____ ¢

5. _____ ¢

6. _____ ¢

Counting Money

Count the money. Write the total on the line.

We write one dollar as $1.00.
We say $1.35 as
one dollar and thirty-five cents.

$1.35

$1.00 = 100¢ $5.00 $10.00 $20.00

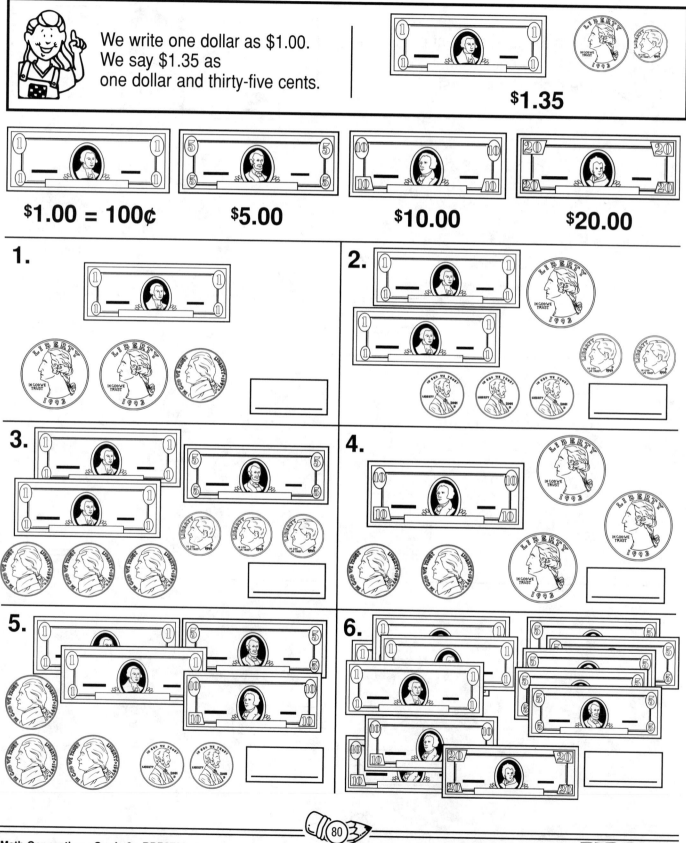

1.

2.

3.

4.

5.

6.

Counting Money

Count the money. Write the total on the line.

Start with the dollars.
Then count the half-dollars,
quarters, dimes, nickels,
and finally, pennies.

I'm saving my money for summer vacation!

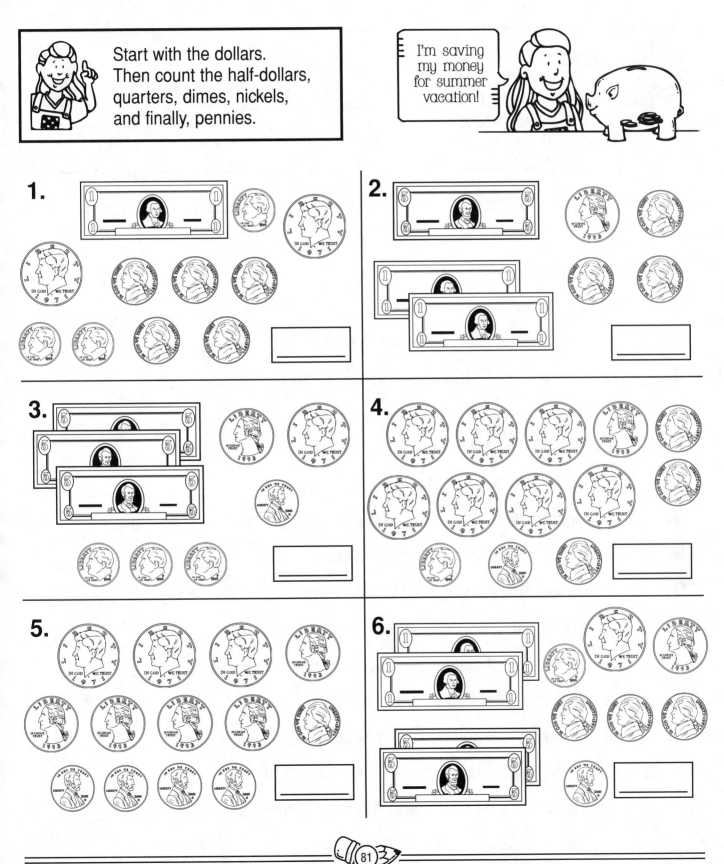

1.

2.

3.

4.

5.

6.

Math Connection—Grade 3—RBP3799

Counting Money

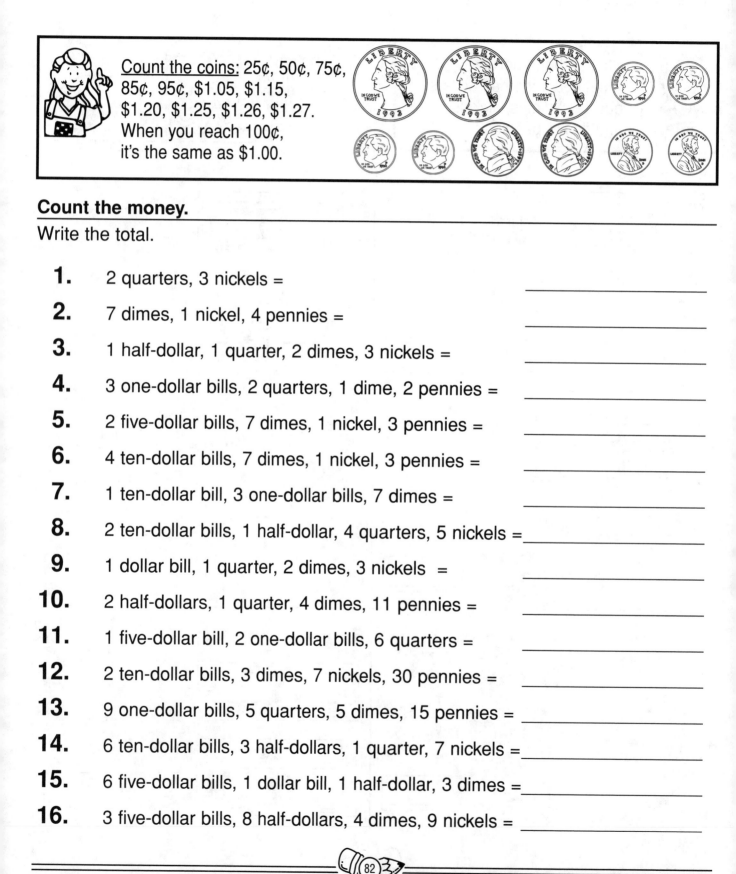

Count the coins: 25¢, 50¢, 75¢, 85¢, 95¢, $1.05, $1.15, $1.20, $1.25, $1.26, $1.27. When you reach 100¢, it's the same as $1.00.

Count the money.

Write the total.

1. 2 quarters, 3 nickels = _____

2. 7 dimes, 1 nickel, 4 pennies = _____

3. 1 half-dollar, 1 quarter, 2 dimes, 3 nickels = _____

4. 3 one-dollar bills, 2 quarters, 1 dime, 2 pennies = _____

5. 2 five-dollar bills, 7 dimes, 1 nickel, 3 pennies = _____

6. 4 ten-dollar bills, 7 dimes, 1 nickel, 3 pennies = _____

7. 1 ten-dollar bill, 3 one-dollar bills, 7 dimes = _____

8. 2 ten-dollar bills, 1 half-dollar, 4 quarters, 5 nickels = _____

9. 1 dollar bill, 1 quarter, 2 dimes, 3 nickels = _____

10. 2 half-dollars, 1 quarter, 4 dimes, 11 pennies = _____

11. 1 five-dollar bill, 2 one-dollar bills, 6 quarters = _____

12. 2 ten-dollar bills, 3 dimes, 7 nickels, 30 pennies = _____

13. 9 one-dollar bills, 5 quarters, 5 dimes, 15 pennies = _____

14. 6 ten-dollar bills, 3 half-dollars, 1 quarter, 7 nickels = _____

15. 6 five-dollar bills, 1 dollar bill, 1 half-dollar, 3 dimes = _____

16. 3 five-dollar bills, 8 half-dollars, 4 dimes, 9 nickels = _____

Money Problem Solving

Solve the problems. Do your work in the box. Write your answer on the line.

Mike wants to buy a game that costs $23.00. He has saved $17.00. How much more does he need to save?	$23.00 − $17.00 **$6.00**

I need to subtract $17.00 from $23.00 to find out how much more. Mike needs $6.00.

---

1. Gina had $17.22.

She earned $5.00 more for helping her mother.

How much did Gina have?

_____

2. Matt had $18.77.

He wanted to buy a CD for $14.50.

How much would he have left after he bought the CD?

_____

---

3. Jon got $3.50 from his mother, $4.00 from his father, and $10.00 from his grandparents.

How much money did Jon get?

_____

4. Len had $53.00.

He was trying to earn enough money for a bike that cost $87.00.

How much more money does he need?

_____

---

5. Dan earned $20.00 for mowing the neighbor's yard.

He already had $12.00.

How much money does he have now?

_____

6. Emma wanted to buy a science kit that cost $18.00.

She only had $6.00.

How much more money does she need?

_____

Money Problem Solving

Solve the problems. Do your work in the box. Write your answer on the line.

When solving a word problem, ask yourself what the question is before trying to solve the problem.

1. Justin had $37.75.

He bought a computer game that cost $25.47.

How much does he have left?

_____

2. Anna earned $12.50 from babysitting on Thursday and $24.00 from babysitting on Friday night.

How much money did she earn altogether?

_____

3. Marcus wanted to buy a trading card that cost $17.00.

He only had $7.49.

How much more did Marcus need?

_____

4. Kaylee saved $86.27.

She received $9.99 from her grandparents for her ninth birthday.

How much money does she have?

_____

5. Dina sold a computer game for $7.00, a CD player for $23.00, and some books for $17.00 at a garage sale.

How much money did she make?

_____

6. Austin had $69.37.

He bought a video game for $39.24 and a CD for $17.39.

How much money does he have left?

_____

Math Connection—Grade 3—RBP3799
www.summerbridgeactivities.com
© RBP Books

Measurement, Money, Time Assessment

Measure the shape in centimeters.

1. What is the measurement of one side?   _____

2. What is the perimeter of the square?   _____

Write the time shown on each clock.

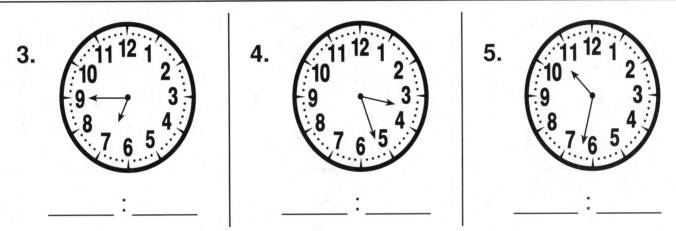

3. _____ : _____

4. _____ : _____

5. _____ : _____

Count the money. Write the total.

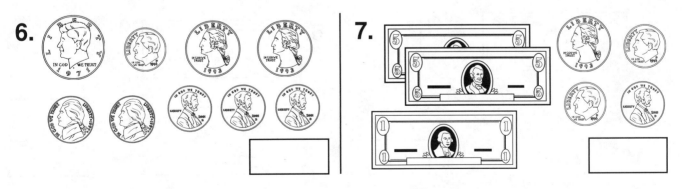

6.

7.

8. Patrick had $7.52. He spent $5.37 on school supplies. How much money did

Patrick have left? _____

Measurement, Money, Time Assessment

Measure the shape in inches.

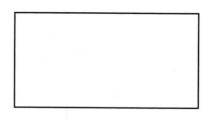

1. What is the measurement of one of the short sides? _____

2. What is the measurement of one of the long sides? _____

3. What is the perimeter of the rectangle? _____

Write the time shown on each clock.

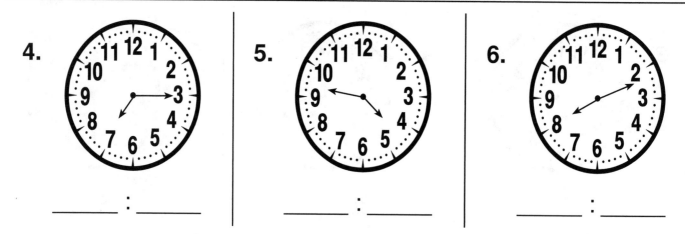

4. _____ : _____

5. _____ : _____

6. _____ : _____

Count the money. Write the total.

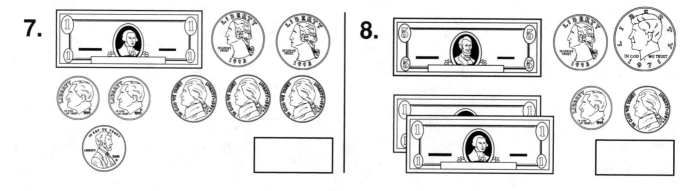

7.

8.

9. Dominick left home at 8:34. It takes him 12 minutes to ride to school. What time did he arrive at school? _____

Reading a Chart

Read the graph. Answer the questions.

 The title of a chart tells you what the chart is about.

Wednesday Night Television Schedule

	7:00	7:30	8:00	8:30	9:00	9:30	10:00	10:30
2	Million Dollar Game Show	Jump Start		News Magazine			News	
4	Lucky Guess	You Should Know	Wednesday Night at the Movies "Friends Forever"				News	
5	Best Friends	Sarah's Secret	Where They Are	Time to Hope	Tom's Talk Show		News	
7	Freakin' Out	Lost Alone	Last One Standing	Sports Tonight			News	
11	Your Health	Eating Right	Nutrition News		Cooking with Kate		Home Decorating	Shopping Show
24	Silly Rabbit	Clyde the Clown	Your Lucky Day	Slime & Rhyme	Cartoon Alley		Fun Times	Make Me Laugh

1. What information does this chart give? _____

2. What time is *Slime & Rhyme* on Channel 24? _____

3. What channel is *Tom's Talk Show* on at 9:00? _____

4. What show is on Channel 11 at 7:30? _____

5. How long is the Wednesday night movie on Channel 4? _____

6. On how many channels can you watch news at 10:00? _____

7. How many shows start at 8:00? _____

8. What would you choose to watch at 9:00? _____

Reading a Chart

Look at the fraction chart. Answer the questions below.

Read the fraction chart across. Each row is equal to 1. The first row has only 1 part, the second row has 2 parts, the third row has 3 parts, and so on.

Fraction Chart

$\frac{1}{1}$							
$\frac{1}{2}$				$\frac{2}{2}$			
$\frac{1}{3}$		$\frac{2}{3}$			$\frac{3}{3}$		
$\frac{1}{4}$		$\frac{2}{4}$		$\frac{3}{4}$		$\frac{4}{4}$	
$\frac{1}{5}$		$\frac{2}{5}$	$\frac{3}{5}$		$\frac{4}{5}$		$\frac{5}{5}$
$\frac{1}{6}$	$\frac{2}{6}$		$\frac{3}{6}$	$\frac{4}{6}$		$\frac{5}{6}$	$\frac{6}{6}$
$\frac{1}{7}$	$\frac{2}{7}$	$\frac{3}{7}$	$\frac{4}{7}$		$\frac{5}{7}$	$\frac{6}{7}$	$\frac{7}{7}$
$\frac{1}{8}$	$\frac{2}{8}$	$\frac{3}{8}$	$\frac{4}{8}$	$\frac{5}{8}$	$\frac{6}{8}$	$\frac{7}{8}$	$\frac{8}{8}$

1. Look at the fifth row. How many fifths equals one whole? _____

2. Which fractions are equal to $\frac{1}{2}$? _____

3. Which fraction is equal to $\frac{1}{3}$? _____

4. Which is larger: $\frac{2}{7}$ or $\frac{3}{6}$? _____

5. Which is smaller: $\frac{7}{8}$ or $\frac{3}{4}$? _____

6. Which fraction is equal to $\frac{3}{4}$? _____

7. Which fraction is larger: $\frac{1}{4}$ or $\frac{2}{6}$? _____

8. Write all the fractions equal to one. _____

Multiplication

Draw a line from the multiplication problem to the way to say it, then to the correct picture.

	2
We read this problem, "two times three equals six." This means: "two groups of three or 3 + 3."	x 3
	6

This exercise is so exciting!

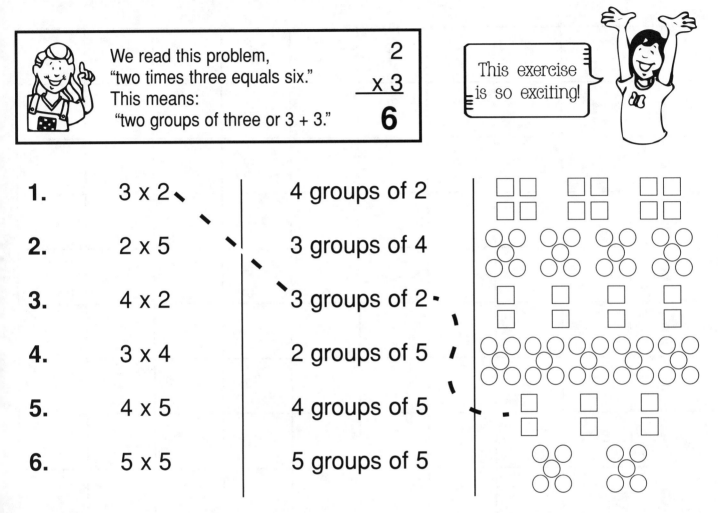

1.	3 x 2	4 groups of 2	
2.	2 x 5	3 groups of 4	
3.	4 x 2	3 groups of 2	
4.	3 x 4	2 groups of 5	
5.	4 x 5	4 groups of 5	
6.	5 x 5	5 groups of 5	

Draw pictures to show the problems.

7.　　4 x 4

8.　　3 x 3

9.　　2 x 6

10.　　4 x 6

Multiplication Chart

Complete the chart; then answer the questions.

x	1	2	3	4	5	6	7	8	9
1	1								
2									
3									
4									
5									
6									
7									
8									
9									

1. What does any number times 1 equal? _____

2. What pattern do you see in the 2s? _____
   _____

3. What pattern do you see in the 5s? _____
   _____

4. Add the digits for each answer in the 9s. What do they each equal? ___

5. 3 x 4 = 12. What does 4 x 3 equal? _____

www.summerbridgeactivities.com

Multiplication Facts 0–3

Solve the problems.

Zero times any number is always 0.	And 1 times any number is the number itself.

1.
$$\begin{array}{r} 1 \\ \times\,9 \\ \hline \end{array}$$
$$\begin{array}{r} 2 \\ \times\,3 \\ \hline \end{array}$$
$$\begin{array}{r} 2 \\ \times\,6 \\ \hline \end{array}$$
$$\begin{array}{r} 3 \\ \times\,7 \\ \hline \end{array}$$
$$\begin{array}{r} 1 \\ \times\,5 \\ \hline \end{array}$$

2.
$$\begin{array}{r} 2 \\ \times\,4 \\ \hline \end{array}$$
$$\begin{array}{r} 3 \\ \times\,3 \\ \hline \end{array}$$
$$\begin{array}{r} 3 \\ \times\,9 \\ \hline \end{array}$$
$$\begin{array}{r} 3 \\ \times\,6 \\ \hline \end{array}$$
$$\begin{array}{r} 2 \\ \times\,2 \\ \hline \end{array}$$

3.
$$\begin{array}{r} 3 \\ \times\,4 \\ \hline \end{array}$$
$$\begin{array}{r} 2 \\ \times\,5 \\ \hline \end{array}$$
$$\begin{array}{r} 1 \\ \times\,4 \\ \hline \end{array}$$
$$\begin{array}{r} 2 \\ \times\,1 \\ \hline \end{array}$$
$$\begin{array}{r} 0 \\ \times\,5 \\ \hline \end{array}$$

4.
$$\begin{array}{r} 2 \\ \times\,8 \\ \hline \end{array}$$
$$\begin{array}{r} 1 \\ \times\,3 \\ \hline \end{array}$$
$$\begin{array}{r} 2 \\ \times\,7 \\ \hline \end{array}$$
$$\begin{array}{r} 3 \\ \times\,8 \\ \hline \end{array}$$
$$\begin{array}{r} 3 \\ \times\,5 \\ \hline \end{array}$$

5.
$$\begin{array}{r} 1 \\ \times\,2 \\ \hline \end{array}$$
$$\begin{array}{r} 1 \\ \times\,7 \\ \hline \end{array}$$
$$\begin{array}{r} 3 \\ \times\,2 \\ \hline \end{array}$$
$$\begin{array}{r} 3 \\ \times\,0 \\ \hline \end{array}$$
$$\begin{array}{r} 1 \\ \times\,6 \\ \hline \end{array}$$

6.
$$\begin{array}{r} 1 \\ \times\,8 \\ \hline \end{array}$$
$$\begin{array}{r} 0 \\ \times\,1 \\ \hline \end{array}$$
$$\begin{array}{r} 1 \\ \times\,1 \\ \hline \end{array}$$
$$\begin{array}{r} 2 \\ \times\,9 \\ \hline \end{array}$$
$$\begin{array}{r} 0 \\ \times\,8 \\ \hline \end{array}$$

www.summerbridgeactivities.com
Math Connection—Grade 3—RBP3799

Multiplication Facts 4–6

Solve the problems.

Learning your basic multiplication facts makes harder math easy! Take the time to memorize your facts.

1.
$$\begin{array}{r} 5 \\ \times\,5 \\ \hline \end{array}$$
$$\begin{array}{r} 6 \\ \times\,8 \\ \hline \end{array}$$
$$\begin{array}{r} 6 \\ \times\,4 \\ \hline \end{array}$$
$$\begin{array}{r} 5 \\ \times\,7 \\ \hline \end{array}$$
$$\begin{array}{r} 6 \\ \times\,6 \\ \hline \end{array}$$

2.
$$\begin{array}{r} 4 \\ \times\,2 \\ \hline \end{array}$$
$$\begin{array}{r} 6 \\ \times\,3 \\ \hline \end{array}$$
$$\begin{array}{r} 5 \\ \times\,4 \\ \hline \end{array}$$
$$\begin{array}{r} 6 \\ \times\,2 \\ \hline \end{array}$$
$$\begin{array}{r} 6 \\ \times\,7 \\ \hline \end{array}$$

3.
$$\begin{array}{r} 4 \\ \times\,3 \\ \hline \end{array}$$
$$\begin{array}{r} 6 \\ \times\,1 \\ \hline \end{array}$$
$$\begin{array}{r} 5 \\ \times\,2 \\ \hline \end{array}$$
$$\begin{array}{r} 5 \\ \times\,0 \\ \hline \end{array}$$
$$\begin{array}{r} 4 \\ \times\,1 \\ \hline \end{array}$$

4.
$$\begin{array}{r} 6 \\ \times\,0 \\ \hline \end{array}$$
$$\begin{array}{r} 5 \\ \times\,6 \\ \hline \end{array}$$
$$\begin{array}{r} 6 \\ \times\,9 \\ \hline \end{array}$$
$$\begin{array}{r} 4 \\ \times\,4 \\ \hline \end{array}$$
$$\begin{array}{r} 5 \\ \times\,3 \\ \hline \end{array}$$

5.
$$\begin{array}{r} 5 \\ \times\,9 \\ \hline \end{array}$$
$$\begin{array}{r} 4 \\ \times\,6 \\ \hline \end{array}$$
$$\begin{array}{r} 5 \\ \times\,8 \\ \hline \end{array}$$
$$\begin{array}{r} 4 \\ \times\,0 \\ \hline \end{array}$$
$$\begin{array}{r} 5 \\ \times\,1 \\ \hline \end{array}$$

6.
$$\begin{array}{r} 4 \\ \times\,5 \\ \hline \end{array}$$
$$\begin{array}{r} 4 \\ \times\,7 \\ \hline \end{array}$$
$$\begin{array}{r} 4 \\ \times\,8 \\ \hline \end{array}$$
$$\begin{array}{r} 6 \\ \times\,5 \\ \hline \end{array}$$
$$\begin{array}{r} 4 \\ \times\,9 \\ \hline \end{array}$$

Multiplication Facts 7–9

Solve the problems.

```
                                        9      6
Notice that the digits of the          x 7    + 3
answers to the 9s add up to 9!         ----   ----
                                        63      9
```

1.
```
   8      7      9      8      7
 x 7    x 3    x 4    x 8    x 1
```

2.
```
   9      8      7      9      8
 x 7    x 5    x 6    x 0    x 2
```

3.
```
   7      8      9      9      7
 x 5    x 3    x 5    x 9    x 2
```

4.
```
   9      8      7      7      9
 x 1    x 4    x 7    x 9    x 6
```

5.
```
   8      7      9      9      8
 x 0    x 4    x 8    x 2    x 1
```

6.
```
   9      8      7      8      0
 x 3    x 6    x 8    x 9    x 7
```

Multiplication Practice

Solve each problem.

1.	2 x 2	3 x 2	5 x 3	1 x 6	6 x 2
2.	2 x 8	5 x 2	2 x 6	2 x 4	2 x 1
3.	7 x 2	3 x 6	9 x 2	8 x 2	4 x 5
4.	3 x 9	6 x 5	4 x 6	3 x 7	8 x 3
5.	4 x 4	5 x 6	5 x 8	7 x 9	8 x 8
6.	5 x 4	8 x 9	7 x 6	5 x 7	4 x 8
7.	6 x 6	7 x 4	8 x 7	9 x 9	9 x 4
8.	4 x 5	5 x 5	5 x 9	6 x 8	4 x 7

Math Connection—Grade 3—RBP3799   www.summerbridgeactivities.com   © RBP Books

Name _____   Date _____

Multiplication Practice

Fill in the charts.

 Try to learn these facts.
Look for patterns.

 ?

1.

Multiply by 6	
9	
5	
3	
6	
7	
4	
2	
8	

2.

Multiply by 8	
9	
5	
3	
6	
7	
4	
2	
8	

3.

Multiply by 3	
9	
5	
3	
6	
7	
4	
2	
8	

4.

Multiply by 7	
9	
5	
3	
6	
7	
4	
2	
8	

5.

Multiply by 5	
9	
5	
3	
6	
7	
4	
2	
8	

6.

Multiply by 9	
9	
5	
3	
6	
7	
4	
2	
8	

7.

Multiply by 4	
9	
5	
3	
6	
7	
4	
2	
8	

8.

Multiply by 1	
9	
5	
3	
6	
7	
4	
2	
8	

9.

Multiply by 2	
9	
5	
3	
6	
7	
4	
2	
8	

www.summerbridgeactivities.com   Math Connection—Grade 3—RBP3799

Multiplication Practice

Complete each wheel below by multiplying from the center out to the edge for each area.

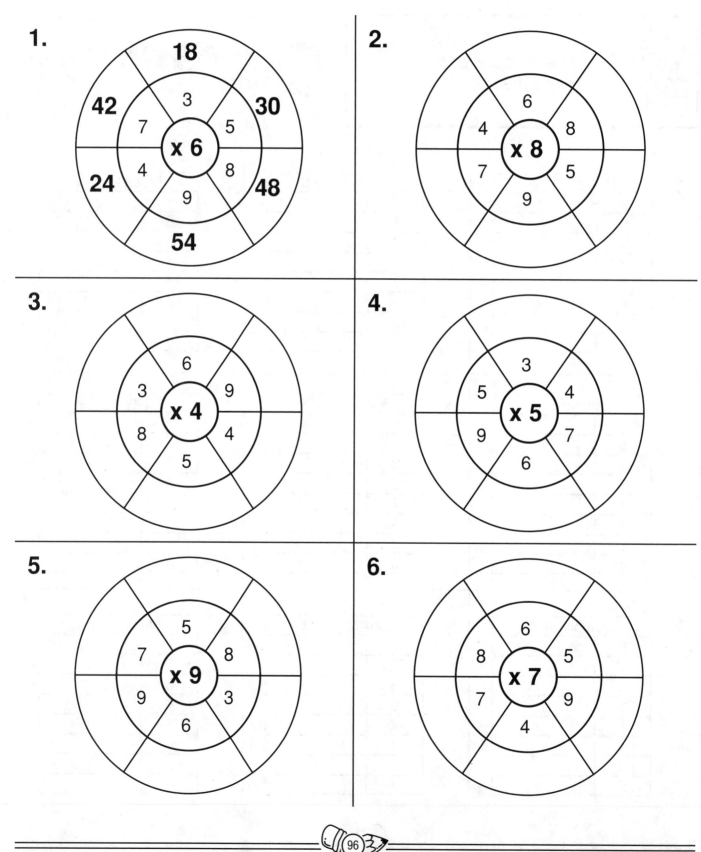

Multiplication Problem Solving

Solve the problems. Do your work in the box. Write your answer on the line.

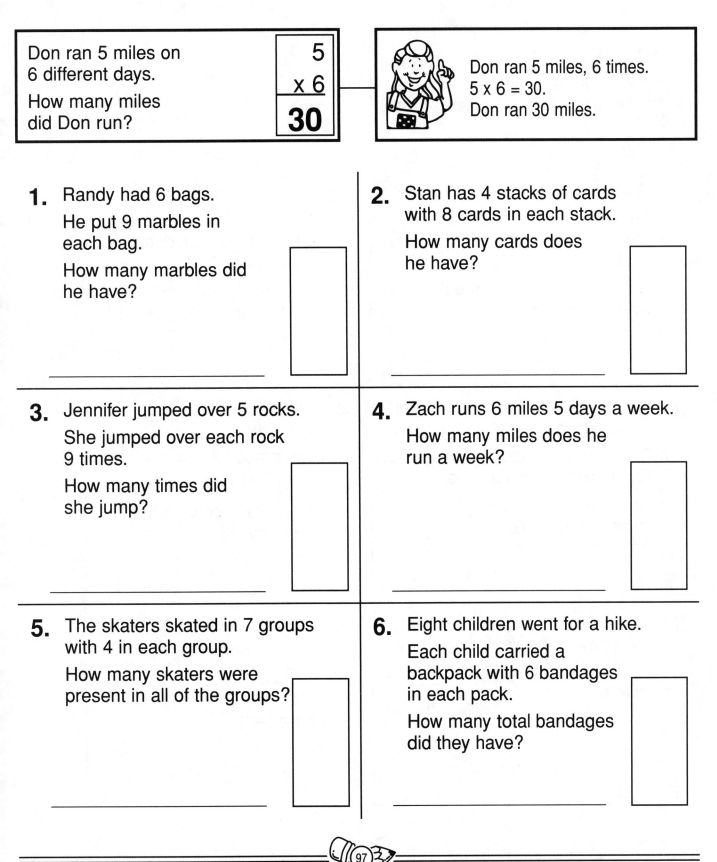

Don ran 5 miles on 6 different days.

How many miles did Don run?

$$\begin{array}{r} 5 \\ \times\ 6 \\ \hline \mathbf{30} \end{array}$$

Don ran 5 miles, 6 times.
5 x 6 = 30.
Don ran 30 miles.

1. Randy had 6 bags.

He put 9 marbles in each bag.

How many marbles did he have?

2. Stan has 4 stacks of cards with 8 cards in each stack.

How many cards does he have?

3. Jennifer jumped over 5 rocks.

She jumped over each rock 9 times.

How many times did she jump?

4. Zach runs 6 miles 5 days a week.

How many miles does he run a week?

5. The skaters skated in 7 groups with 4 in each group.

How many skaters were present in all of the groups?

6. Eight children went for a hike.

Each child carried a backpack with 6 bandages in each pack.

How many total bandages did they have?

Multiplication Problem Solving

Solve the problems. Do your work in the box. Write your answer on the line.

Be sure to know the question you are answering. Write the answer so that it makes sense.

1. The store display had 9 shelves.

The stock boy placed 9 boxes of cereal on each shelf.

How many boxes of cereal were on display?

_____

2. The third graders formed 8 relay teams.

There were 7 students on each team.

How many students were running in the relay?

_____

3. Mrs. Martinez made a scrapbook for her daughter.

The scrapbook had 7 pages. Each page had 6 pictures.

How many pictures were in the scrapbook?

_____

4. John keeps his baseball cards in a notebook.

His notebook has 8 pages.

Each page has 9 cards.

How many cards does John have?

_____

5. Jenna wrote 2 pages in her diary each day of the week.

How many pages did she write each week?

_____

6. Carlos has 5 jars of marbles.

He has 8 marbles in each jar.

How many marbles does he have?

_____

Math Connection—Grade 3—RBP3799   www.summerbridgeactivities.com   © RBP Books

Division

Solve the problems. Draw pictures to show your thinking.

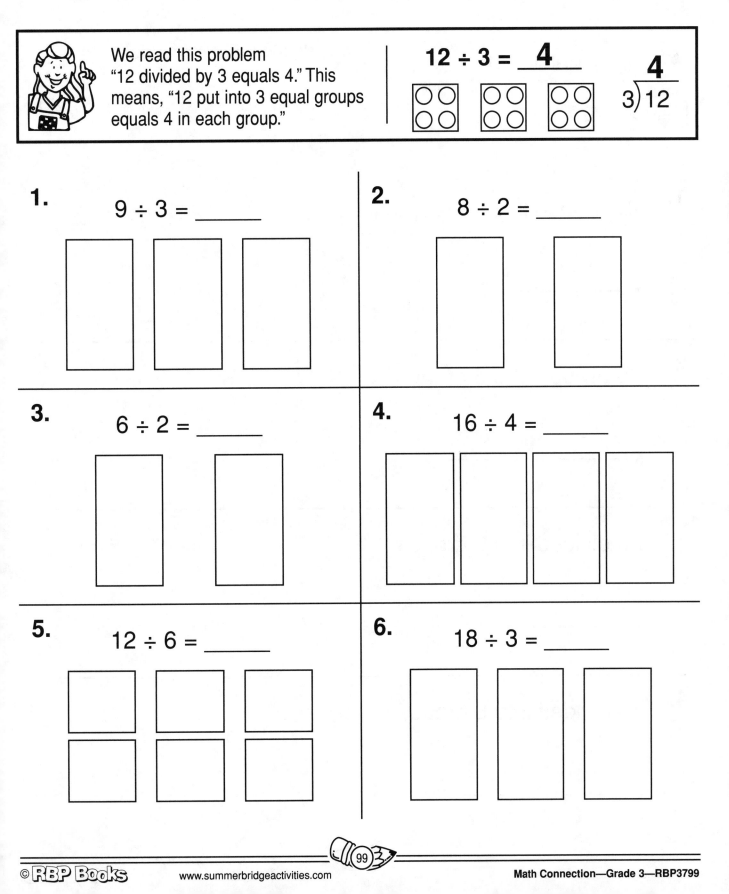

We read this problem "12 divided by 3 equals 4." This means, "12 put into 3 equal groups equals 4 in each group."

$12 \div 3 = \underline{\quad 4 \quad}$

$3\overline{)12}$ → 4

1. $9 \div 3 = \underline{\hspace{1cm}}$

2. $8 \div 2 = \underline{\hspace{1cm}}$

3. $6 \div 2 = \underline{\hspace{1cm}}$

4. $16 \div 4 = \underline{\hspace{1cm}}$

5. $12 \div 6 = \underline{\hspace{1cm}}$

6. $18 \div 3 = \underline{\hspace{1cm}}$

www.summerbridgeactivities.com   Math Connection—Grade 3—RBP3799

Division

Solve the problems. Draw a picture and write the equation.

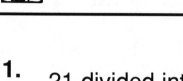

20 total are put into 4 groups.
There are 5 in each group.

20 ÷ 4 = 5

20 divided into 4 groups

$$4\overline{)20} = 5$$

---

1. 21 divided into 3 groups

_____

2. 30 divided into 5 groups

_____

3. 36 divided into 9 groups

_____

4. 18 divided into 6 groups

_____

Division Practice

Solve each problem.

> Keep practicing until you know all your facts.

1.
2 ÷ 2 = _____
4 ÷ 2 = _____
6 ÷ 2 = _____
8 ÷ 2 = _____
10 ÷ 2 = _____
12 ÷ 2 = _____
14 ÷ 2 = _____
16 ÷ 2 = _____
18 ÷ 2 = _____
20 ÷ 2 = _____

2.
3 ÷ 3 = _____
9 ÷ 3 = _____
15 ÷ 3 = _____
21 ÷ 3 = _____
27 ÷ 3 = _____
6 ÷ 3 = _____
12 ÷ 3 = _____
18 ÷ 3 = _____
24 ÷ 3 = _____
30 ÷ 3 = _____

3.
4 ÷ 4 = _____
8 ÷ 4 = _____
16 ÷ 4 = _____
24 ÷ 4 = _____
32 ÷ 4 = _____
40 ÷ 4 = _____
12 ÷ 4 = _____
20 ÷ 4 = _____
28 ÷ 4 = _____
36 ÷ 4 = _____

4.
5 ÷ 5 = _____
15 ÷ 5 = _____
30 ÷ 5 = _____
45 ÷ 5 = _____
40 ÷ 5 = _____
25 ÷ 5 = _____
10 ÷ 5 = _____
35 ÷ 5 = _____
50 ÷ 5 = _____
20 ÷ 5 = _____

5.
6 ÷ 6 = _____
12 ÷ 6 = _____
54 ÷ 6 = _____
18 ÷ 6 = _____
48 ÷ 6 = _____
24 ÷ 6 = _____
60 ÷ 6 = _____
42 ÷ 6 = _____
36 ÷ 6 = _____
30 ÷ 6 = _____

6.
7 ÷ 7 = _____
14 ÷ 7 = _____
28 ÷ 7 = _____
42 ÷ 7 = _____
70 ÷ 7 = _____
56 ÷ 7 = _____
21 ÷ 7 = _____
35 ÷ 7 = _____
49 ÷ 7 = _____
63 ÷ 7 = _____

www.summerbridgeactivities.com
Math Connection—Grade 3—RBP3799

Division Practice
Solve each problem.

1. $6 \div 2 =$ _____

$6 \div 3 =$ _____

2. $12 \div 3 =$ _____

$12 \div 4 =$ _____

3. $15 \div 5 =$ _____

$15 \div 3 =$ _____

4. $10 \div 5 =$ _____

$10 \div 2 =$ _____

5. $16 \div 2 =$ _____

$16 \div 8 =$ _____

6. $20 \div 4 =$ _____

$20 \div 5 =$ _____

7. $24 \div 6 =$ _____

$24 \div 4 =$ _____

8. $28 \div 4 =$ _____

$28 \div 7 =$ _____

9. $36 \div 9 =$ _____

$36 \div 4 =$ _____

10. $16 \div 8 =$ _____

$16 \div 2 =$ _____

11. $48 \div 6 =$ _____

$48 \div 8 =$ _____

12. $54 \div 9 =$ _____

$54 \div 6 =$ _____

13. $5 \overline{)40}$ $\quad$ $6 \overline{)42}$ $\quad$ $3 \overline{)27}$ $\quad$ $2 \overline{)16}$

14. $7 \overline{)49}$ $\quad$ $8 \overline{)56}$ $\quad$ $4 \overline{)16}$ $\quad$ $9 \overline{)45}$

15. $10 \overline{)90}$ $\quad$ $6 \overline{)48}$ $\quad$ $7 \overline{)56}$ $\quad$ $9 \overline{)36}$

16. $5 \overline{)30}$ $\quad$ $8 \overline{)72}$ $\quad$ $9 \overline{)63}$ $\quad$ $7 \overline{)42}$

Math Connection—Grade 3—RBP3799

Division Practice

Solve each problem.

> Knowing your multiplication facts makes these division problems a snap!

1. $6\overline{)36}$ $7\overline{)42}$ $8\overline{)56}$ $5\overline{)45}$

2. $3\overline{)21}$ $9\overline{)63}$ $4\overline{)36}$ $6\overline{)54}$

3. $5\overline{)35}$ $3\overline{)27}$ $2\overline{)18}$ $7\overline{)49}$

4. $3\overline{)18}$ $6\overline{)24}$ $4\overline{)32}$ $9\overline{)54}$

5. $4\overline{)16}$ $2\overline{)14}$ $5\overline{)25}$ $8\overline{)64}$

6. $9\overline{)36}$ $4\overline{)24}$ $7\overline{)35}$ $5\overline{)30}$

7. $6\overline{)42}$ $2\overline{)16}$ $6\overline{)24}$ $5\overline{)40}$

8. $3\overline{)24}$ $7\overline{)21}$ $8\overline{)72}$ $9\overline{)81}$

Division Problem Solving

Solve the problems. Do your work in the box. Write your answer on the line.

| Brian has 15 dog treats. He has 3 dogs. How many dog treats can each dog get? | There are 15 in all. 15 is the <u>dividend</u>. He has 3 dogs. 3 is the <u>divisor</u>. The answer is 5. 5 is the <u>quotient</u>. $\begin{array}{r} 5 \\ 3\overline{)15} \end{array}$ |

1. David has 12 goldfish.

He has 2 fish tanks.

How many goldfish will be in each tank if he divides them evenly?

_____

2. Deb bought 8 new bracelets.

She will wear the same number on each wrist.

How many will she have on each wrist?

_____

3. Sam's team scored 16 points.

They scored the same number of points in each of the 4 quarters.

How many points did they score in each quarter?

_____

4. Nick has 15 trophies.

He displays them evenly on 3 shelves.

How many trophies are on each shelf?

_____

5. Jan has 18 buttons. She has 6 pockets on her pants. She sewed the same number of buttons on each pocket.

How many buttons did she sew on each pocket?

_____

6. Kelly has 35 new photos to add to her album. She will put 7 photos on each page.

How many pages will she need?

_____

Division Problem Solving

Solve the problems. Do your work in the box. Write your answer on the line.

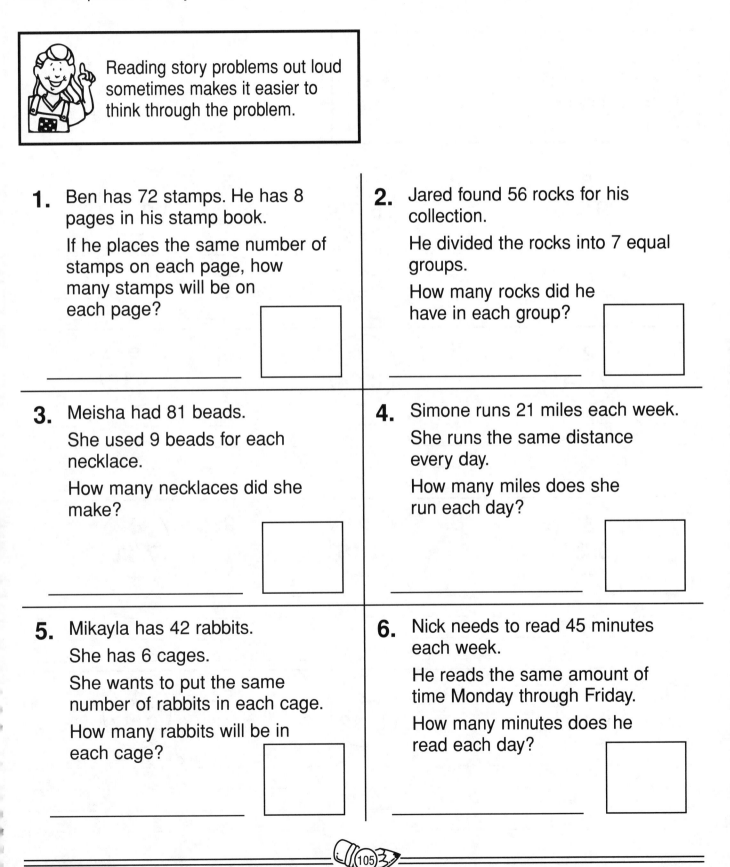

Reading story problems out loud sometimes makes it easier to think through the problem.

1. Ben has 72 stamps. He has 8 pages in his stamp book.

If he places the same number of stamps on each page, how many stamps will be on each page?

_____

2. Jared found 56 rocks for his collection.

He divided the rocks into 7 equal groups.

How many rocks did he have in each group?

_____

3. Meisha had 81 beads.

She used 9 beads for each necklace.

How many necklaces did she make?

_____

4. Simone runs 21 miles each week.

She runs the same distance every day.

How many miles does she run each day?

_____

5. Mikayla has 42 rabbits.

She has 6 cages.

She wants to put the same number of rabbits in each cage.

How many rabbits will be in each cage?

_____

6. Nick needs to read 45 minutes each week.

He reads the same amount of time Monday through Friday.

How many minutes does he read each day?

_____

Multiplication and Division Fact Families

Create different equations using each member of the fact families.

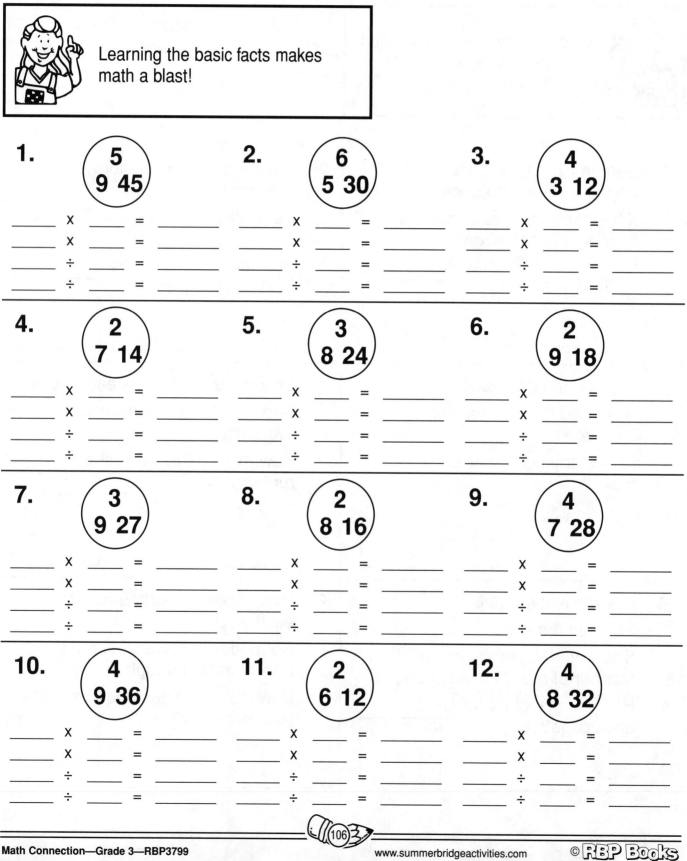

Learning the basic facts makes math a blast!

1. (5 9 45)

_____ x _____ = _____
_____ x _____ = _____
_____ ÷ _____ = _____
_____ ÷ _____ = _____

2. (6 5 30)

_____ x _____ = _____
_____ x _____ = _____
_____ ÷ _____ = _____
_____ ÷ _____ = _____

3. (4 3 12)

_____ x _____ = _____
_____ x _____ = _____
_____ ÷ _____ = _____
_____ ÷ _____ = _____

4. (2 7 14)

_____ x _____ = _____
_____ x _____ = _____
_____ ÷ _____ = _____
_____ ÷ _____ = _____

5. (3 8 24)

_____ x _____ = _____
_____ x _____ = _____
_____ ÷ _____ = _____
_____ ÷ _____ = _____

6. (2 9 18)

_____ x _____ = _____
_____ x _____ = _____
_____ ÷ _____ = _____
_____ ÷ _____ = _____

7. (3 9 27)

_____ x _____ = _____
_____ x _____ = _____
_____ ÷ _____ = _____
_____ ÷ _____ = _____

8. (2 8 16)

_____ x _____ = _____
_____ x _____ = _____
_____ ÷ _____ = _____
_____ ÷ _____ = _____

9. (4 7 28)

_____ x _____ = _____
_____ x _____ = _____
_____ ÷ _____ = _____
_____ ÷ _____ = _____

10. (4 9 36)

_____ x _____ = _____
_____ x _____ = _____
_____ ÷ _____ = _____
_____ ÷ _____ = _____

11. (2 6 12)

_____ x _____ = _____
_____ x _____ = _____
_____ ÷ _____ = _____
_____ ÷ _____ = _____

12. (4 8 32)

_____ x _____ = _____
_____ x _____ = _____
_____ ÷ _____ = _____
_____ ÷ _____ = _____

Math Connection—Grade 3—RBP3799   www.summerbridgeactivities.com   © RBP Books

Multiplication and Division Fact Families

Create different equations using each member of the fact families.

Just like addition and subtraction facts, multiplication and division facts are related.

Fact Families

6 24 4

1.

(7 / 8 56)

7	x	8	=	56
8	x	7	=	56
56	÷	8	=	7
56	÷	7	=	8

(6 / 7 42)

_____ x _____ = _____
_____ x _____ = _____
_____ ÷ _____ = _____
_____ ÷ _____ = _____

(4 / 5 20)

_____ x _____ = _____
_____ x _____ = _____
_____ ÷ _____ = _____
_____ ÷ _____ = _____

2.

(9 / 8 72)

_____ x _____ = _____
_____ x _____ = _____
_____ ÷ _____ = _____
_____ ÷ _____ = _____

(9 / 7 63)

_____ x _____ = _____
_____ x _____ = _____
_____ ÷ _____ = _____
_____ ÷ _____ = _____

(9 / 6 54)

_____ x _____ = _____
_____ x _____ = _____
_____ ÷ _____ = _____
_____ ÷ _____ = _____

3.

(7 / 7 49)

_____ x _____ = _____
_____ ÷ _____ = _____

(8 / 8 64)

_____ x _____ = _____
_____ ÷ _____ = _____

(9 / 9 81)

_____ x _____ = _____
_____ ÷ _____ = _____

4.

(6 / 8 48)

_____ x _____ = _____
_____ x _____ = _____
_____ ÷ _____ = _____
_____ ÷ _____ = _____

(4 / 8 32)

_____ x _____ = _____
_____ x _____ = _____
_____ ÷ _____ = _____
_____ ÷ _____ = _____

(4 / 9 36)

_____ x _____ = _____
_____ x _____ = _____
_____ ÷ _____ = _____
_____ ÷ _____ = _____

www.summerbridgeactivities.com

Math Connection—Grade 3—RBP3799

Multiplication and Division Assessment

Solve each problem.

1.
$$\begin{array}{r} 6 \\ \times\,8 \\ \hline \end{array}\qquad \begin{array}{r} 7 \\ \times\,3 \\ \hline \end{array}\qquad \begin{array}{r} 8 \\ \times\,2 \\ \hline \end{array}\qquad \begin{array}{r} 9 \\ \times\,4 \\ \hline \end{array}\qquad \begin{array}{r} 2 \\ \times\,7 \\ \hline \end{array}$$

2.
$$\begin{array}{r} 4 \\ \times\,9 \\ \hline \end{array}\qquad \begin{array}{r} 3 \\ \times\,8 \\ \hline \end{array}\qquad \begin{array}{r} 4 \\ \times\,4 \\ \hline \end{array}\qquad \begin{array}{r} 6 \\ \times\,2 \\ \hline \end{array}\qquad \begin{array}{r} 3 \\ \times\,5 \\ \hline \end{array}$$

3.
$$\begin{array}{r} 8 \\ \times\,8 \\ \hline \end{array}\qquad \begin{array}{r} 6 \\ \times\,5 \\ \hline \end{array}\qquad \begin{array}{r} 2 \\ \times\,3 \\ \hline \end{array}\qquad \begin{array}{r} 4 \\ \times\,7 \\ \hline \end{array}\qquad \begin{array}{r} 2 \\ \times\,9 \\ \hline \end{array}$$

4.
$$\begin{array}{r} 5 \\ \times\,6 \\ \hline \end{array}\qquad \begin{array}{r} 8 \\ \times\,7 \\ \hline \end{array}\qquad \begin{array}{r} 4 \\ \times\,5 \\ \hline \end{array}\qquad \begin{array}{r} 7 \\ \times\,7 \\ \hline \end{array}\qquad \begin{array}{r} 9 \\ \times\,8 \\ \hline \end{array}$$

5. $9\overline{)81}$ $\qquad$ $7\overline{)35}$ $\qquad$ $4\overline{)32}$ $\qquad$ $6\overline{)48}$

6. $5\overline{)45}$ $\qquad$ $4\overline{)24}$ $\qquad$ $9\overline{)63}$ $\qquad$ $8\overline{)56}$

7. $9\overline{)72}$ $\qquad$ $7\overline{)42}$ $\qquad$ $6\overline{)18}$ $\qquad$ $3\overline{)21}$

8. $8\overline{)40}$ $\qquad$ $6\overline{)54}$ $\qquad$ $8\overline{)64}$ $\qquad$ $9\overline{)36}$

Math Connection—Grade 3—RBP3799   www.summerbridgeactivities.com   © RBP Books

Multiplication and Division Assessment

Solve each problem.

1. $\begin{array}{r} 5 \\ \times\,8 \\ \hline \end{array}$ $\begin{array}{r} 7 \\ \times\,4 \\ \hline \end{array}$ $\begin{array}{r} 8 \\ \times\,3 \\ \hline \end{array}$ $\begin{array}{r} 9 \\ \times\,7 \\ \hline \end{array}$ $\begin{array}{r} 6 \\ \times\,7 \\ \hline \end{array}$

2. $\begin{array}{r} 4 \\ \times\,8 \\ \hline \end{array}$ $\begin{array}{r} 7 \\ \times\,8 \\ \hline \end{array}$ $\begin{array}{r} 5 \\ \times\,5 \\ \hline \end{array}$ $\begin{array}{r} 6 \\ \times\,4 \\ \hline \end{array}$ $\begin{array}{r} 3 \\ \times\,3 \\ \hline \end{array}$

3. $\begin{array}{r} 9 \\ \times\,8 \\ \hline \end{array}$ $\begin{array}{r} 8 \\ \times\,5 \\ \hline \end{array}$ $\begin{array}{r} 2 \\ \times\,8 \\ \hline \end{array}$ $\begin{array}{r} 6 \\ \times\,7 \\ \hline \end{array}$ $\begin{array}{r} 2 \\ \times\,6 \\ \hline \end{array}$

4. $\begin{array}{r} 7 \\ \times\,5 \\ \hline \end{array}$ $\begin{array}{r} 8 \\ \times\,6 \\ \hline \end{array}$ $\begin{array}{r} 7 \\ \times\,9 \\ \hline \end{array}$ $\begin{array}{r} 6 \\ \times\,6 \\ \hline \end{array}$ $\begin{array}{r} 8 \\ \times\,9 \\ \hline \end{array}$

5. $8\overline{)16}$ $6\overline{)36}$ $5\overline{)35}$ $6\overline{)42}$

6. $8\overline{)40}$ $7\overline{)21}$ $6\overline{)24}$ $9\overline{)54}$

7. $8\overline{)72}$ $7\overline{)49}$ $4\overline{)28}$ $9\overline{)27}$

8. $5\overline{)30}$ $6\overline{)12}$ $8\overline{)56}$ $9\overline{)63}$

Multiplication by Tens
Look for a pattern.

Look for a pattern.

Any number times 10 is that number with a 0 at the end.
Finding the pattern helps me do these in my head.

2	22	3	35	88
x 10	x 10	x 10	x 10	x 10
20	**220**	**30**	**350**	**880**

1.
24	33	77	9	3
x 10	x 10	x 10	x 10	x 10

2.
4	44	7	42	72
x 10	x 10	x 10	x 10	x 10

3.
28	86	51	29	82
x 10	x 10	x 10	x 10	x 10

4.
8	23	66	83	13
x 10	x 10	x 10	x 10	x 10

5.
17	35	42	18	99
x 10	x 10	x 10	x 10	x 10

6.
6	70	89	41	20
x 10	x 10	x 10	x 10	x 10

Math Connection—Grade 3—RBP3799   www.summerbridgeactivities.com   © RBP Books

2-Digit Multiplication

Solve each problem.

First multiply the ones.
Then multiply the tens.
Add.

Shortcut:

$$\begin{array}{r} 1\ 2 \\ \times\ \ 3 \\ \hline 3\ 6 \end{array}$$

$$\begin{array}{r} 1\ 2 \\ \times\ \ 3 \\ \hline 6 \end{array}$$
$+$
$$\begin{array}{r} 1\ 2 \\ \times\ \ 3 \\ \hline 3\ 0 \end{array} = 36$$

Multiply the ones.
Multiply the tens.

1.
$$\begin{array}{r} 12 \\ \times\ 4 \end{array}$$
$$\begin{array}{r} 11 \\ \times\ 2 \end{array}$$
$$\begin{array}{r} 13 \\ \times\ 2 \end{array}$$
$$\begin{array}{r} 13 \\ \times\ 3 \end{array}$$

2.
$$\begin{array}{r} 11 \\ \times\ 3 \end{array}$$
$$\begin{array}{r} 14 \\ \times\ 2 \end{array}$$
$$\begin{array}{r} 12 \\ \times\ 3 \end{array}$$
$$\begin{array}{r} 11 \\ \times\ 4 \end{array}$$

3.
$$\begin{array}{r} 13 \\ \times\ 1 \end{array}$$
$$\begin{array}{r} 11 \\ \times\ 6 \end{array}$$
$$\begin{array}{r} 22 \\ \times\ 3 \end{array}$$
$$\begin{array}{r} 32 \\ \times\ 2 \end{array}$$

4.
$$\begin{array}{r} 42 \\ \times\ 2 \end{array}$$
$$\begin{array}{r} 24 \\ \times\ 2 \end{array}$$
$$\begin{array}{r} 22 \\ \times\ 2 \end{array}$$
$$\begin{array}{r} 21 \\ \times\ 3 \end{array}$$

5.
$$\begin{array}{r} 33 \\ \times\ 3 \end{array}$$
$$\begin{array}{r} 32 \\ \times\ 3 \end{array}$$
$$\begin{array}{r} 31 \\ \times\ 3 \end{array}$$
$$\begin{array}{r} 31 \\ \times\ 2 \end{array}$$

2-Digit Multiplication
Solve each problem.

 Remember to multiply the ones first, then the tens. It's just like addition and subtraction. Always start with the ones.

1.
$$\begin{array}{r} 10 \\ \times\ 7 \\ \hline \end{array}$$
$$\begin{array}{r} 11 \\ \times\ 7 \\ \hline \end{array}$$
$$\begin{array}{r} 14 \\ \times\ 1 \\ \hline \end{array}$$
$$\begin{array}{r} 20 \\ \times\ 4 \\ \hline \end{array}$$

2.
$$\begin{array}{r} 22 \\ \times\ 4 \\ \hline \end{array}$$
$$\begin{array}{r} 23 \\ \times\ 2 \\ \hline \end{array}$$
$$\begin{array}{r} 12 \\ \times\ 3 \\ \hline \end{array}$$
$$\begin{array}{r} 21 \\ \times\ 4 \\ \hline \end{array}$$

3.
$$\begin{array}{r} 23 \\ \times\ 1 \\ \hline \end{array}$$
$$\begin{array}{r} 11 \\ \times\ 8 \\ \hline \end{array}$$
$$\begin{array}{r} 33 \\ \times\ 2 \\ \hline \end{array}$$
$$\begin{array}{r} 65 \\ \times\ 1 \\ \hline \end{array}$$

4.
$$\begin{array}{r} 44 \\ \times\ 2 \\ \hline \end{array}$$
$$\begin{array}{r} 20 \\ \times\ 4 \\ \hline \end{array}$$
$$\begin{array}{r} 21 \\ \times\ 2 \\ \hline \end{array}$$
$$\begin{array}{r} 11 \\ \times\ 9 \\ \hline \end{array}$$

5.
$$\begin{array}{r} 11 \\ \times\ 5 \\ \hline \end{array}$$
$$\begin{array}{r} 15 \\ \times\ 1 \\ \hline \end{array}$$
$$\begin{array}{r} 22 \\ \times\ 3 \\ \hline \end{array}$$
$$\begin{array}{r} 30 \\ \times\ 2 \\ \hline \end{array}$$

6.
$$\begin{array}{r} 40 \\ \times\ 2 \\ \hline \end{array}$$
$$\begin{array}{r} 41 \\ \times\ 2 \\ \hline \end{array}$$
$$\begin{array}{r} 78 \\ \times\ 1 \\ \hline \end{array}$$
$$\begin{array}{r} 32 \\ \times\ 3 \\ \hline \end{array}$$

Math Connection—Grade 3—RBP3799

www.summerbridgeactivities.com

2-Digit Multiplication with Regrouping
Solve each problem.

Multiply the ones.
Multiply the tens.
Add.

Shortcut:
Multiply the ones.
Carry the ten over
the tens.

$$\begin{array}{r} {}^{1}1\ 3 \\ \times\ \ \ 6 \\ \hline 7\ 8 \end{array}$$

$$\begin{array}{r} 1\ 3 \\ \times\ \ \ 6 \\ \hline 1\ 8 \end{array} + \begin{array}{r} 1\ \ 3 \\ \times\ \ \ \ 6 \\ \hline 6\ 0 \end{array} = 78$$

Multiply the tens.
$6 \times 10 = 60$
Add the extra ten.
$60 + 10 = 70$

1.	15	14	13	24	22
	x 6	x 5	x 7	x 3	x 5

2.	12	25	32	23	14
	x 7	x 4	x 6	x 7	x 8

3.	26	52	44	34	13
	x 3	x 6	x 5	x 6	x 9

4.	84	45	32	16	28
	x 3	x 6	x 9	x 7	x 2

5.	35	18	22	34	47
	x 6	x 7	x 7	x 5	x 3

6.	19	33	42	63	83
	x 2	x 6	x 8	x 4	x 5

www.summerbridgeactivities.com **Math Connection—Grade 3—RBP3799**

2-Digit Multiplication with Regrouping

Solve each problem.

1. 13 x 6	18 x 9	22 x 8	29 x 6	39 x 5	22 x 9
2. 48 x 5	56 x 3	72 x 9	25 x 7	36 x 4	43 x 7
3. 16 x 6	27 x 8	66 x 2	43 x 9	37 x 6	87 x 2
4. 26 x 6	29 x 4	32 x 8	14 x 7	63 x 5	73 x 8
5. 58 x 5	18 x 6	27 x 4	62 x 6	37 x 3	53 x 9
6. 67 x 5	23 x 8	13 x 5	45 x 7	44 x 6	54 x 7
7. 84 x 6	26 x 9	29 x 8	34 x 9	55 x 2	93 x 4

Math Connection—Grade 3—RBP3799   www.summerbridgeactivities.com   © RBP Books

2-Digit Multiplication with Regrouping

Solve each problem.

1.
$$\begin{array}{r} 25 \\ \times\ 6 \\ \hline \end{array} \qquad \begin{array}{r} 16 \\ \times\ 9 \\ \hline \end{array} \qquad \begin{array}{r} 46 \\ \times\ 8 \\ \hline \end{array} \qquad \begin{array}{r} 64 \\ \times\ 7 \\ \hline \end{array} \qquad \begin{array}{r} 85 \\ \times\ 4 \\ \hline \end{array} \qquad \begin{array}{r} 63 \\ \times\ 6 \\ \hline \end{array} \qquad \begin{array}{r} 32 \\ \times\ 7 \\ \hline \end{array}$$

2.
$$\begin{array}{r} 18 \\ \times\ 5 \\ \hline \end{array} \qquad \begin{array}{r} 43 \\ \times\ 8 \\ \hline \end{array} \qquad \begin{array}{r} 54 \\ \times\ 5 \\ \hline \end{array} \qquad \begin{array}{r} 27 \\ \times\ 6 \\ \hline \end{array} \qquad \begin{array}{r} 14 \\ \times\ 9 \\ \hline \end{array} \qquad \begin{array}{r} 64 \\ \times\ 8 \\ \hline \end{array} \qquad \begin{array}{r} 55 \\ \times\ 3 \\ \hline \end{array}$$

3.
$$\begin{array}{r} 36 \\ \times\ 9 \\ \hline \end{array} \qquad \begin{array}{r} 29 \\ \times\ 5 \\ \hline \end{array} \qquad \begin{array}{r} 41 \\ \times\ 8 \\ \hline \end{array} \qquad \begin{array}{r} 66 \\ \times\ 4 \\ \hline \end{array} \qquad \begin{array}{r} 73 \\ \times\ 5 \\ \hline \end{array} \qquad \begin{array}{r} 27 \\ \times\ 3 \\ \hline \end{array} \qquad \begin{array}{r} 17 \\ \times\ 8 \\ \hline \end{array}$$

4.
$$\begin{array}{r} 44 \\ \times\ 7 \\ \hline \end{array} \qquad \begin{array}{r} 68 \\ \times\ 5 \\ \hline \end{array} \qquad \begin{array}{r} 94 \\ \times\ 4 \\ \hline \end{array} \qquad \begin{array}{r} 74 \\ \times\ 7 \\ \hline \end{array} \qquad \begin{array}{r} 58 \\ \times\ 6 \\ \hline \end{array} \qquad \begin{array}{r} 25 \\ \times\ 8 \\ \hline \end{array} \qquad \begin{array}{r} 16 \\ \times\ 4 \\ \hline \end{array}$$

5.
$$\begin{array}{r} 27 \\ \times\ 5 \\ \hline \end{array} \qquad \begin{array}{r} 48 \\ \times\ 4 \\ \hline \end{array} \qquad \begin{array}{r} 66 \\ \times\ 7 \\ \hline \end{array} \qquad \begin{array}{r} 97 \\ \times\ 5 \\ \hline \end{array} \qquad \begin{array}{r} 55 \\ \times\ 6 \\ \hline \end{array} \qquad \begin{array}{r} 18 \\ \times\ 8 \\ \hline \end{array} \qquad \begin{array}{r} 78 \\ \times\ 4 \\ \hline \end{array}$$

6.
$$\begin{array}{r} 34 \\ \times\ 7 \\ \hline \end{array} \qquad \begin{array}{r} 27 \\ \times\ 2 \\ \hline \end{array} \qquad \begin{array}{r} 93 \\ \times\ 6 \\ \hline \end{array} \qquad \begin{array}{r} 52 \\ \times\ 5 \\ \hline \end{array} \qquad \begin{array}{r} 38 \\ \times\ 4 \\ \hline \end{array} \qquad \begin{array}{r} 46 \\ \times\ 6 \\ \hline \end{array} \qquad \begin{array}{r} 32 \\ \times\ 5 \\ \hline \end{array}$$

7.
$$\begin{array}{r} 98 \\ \times\ 3 \\ \hline \end{array} \qquad \begin{array}{r} 72 \\ \times\ 7 \\ \hline \end{array} \qquad \begin{array}{r} 63 \\ \times\ 9 \\ \hline \end{array} \qquad \begin{array}{r} 44 \\ \times\ 8 \\ \hline \end{array} \qquad \begin{array}{r} 56 \\ \times\ 7 \\ \hline \end{array} \qquad \begin{array}{r} 26 \\ \times\ 5 \\ \hline \end{array} \qquad \begin{array}{r} 15 \\ \times\ 8 \\ \hline \end{array}$$

www.summerbridgeactivities.com   **Math Connection—Grade 3—RBP3799**

2-Digit Multiplication with Regrouping

Solve each problem.

1.
$$\begin{array}{r} 59 \\ \times\ 6 \\ \hline \end{array} \qquad \begin{array}{r} 18 \\ \times\ 5 \\ \hline \end{array} \qquad \begin{array}{r} 62 \\ \times\ 7 \\ \hline \end{array} \qquad \begin{array}{r} 45 \\ \times\ 9 \\ \hline \end{array} \qquad \begin{array}{r} 69 \\ \times\ 8 \\ \hline \end{array} \qquad \begin{array}{r} 23 \\ \times\ 9 \\ \hline \end{array} \qquad \begin{array}{r} 28 \\ \times\ 7 \\ \hline \end{array}$$

2.
$$\begin{array}{r} 66 \\ \times\ 5 \\ \hline \end{array} \qquad \begin{array}{r} 34 \\ \times\ 8 \\ \hline \end{array} \qquad \begin{array}{r} 42 \\ \times\ 9 \\ \hline \end{array} \qquad \begin{array}{r} 65 \\ \times\ 7 \\ \hline \end{array} \qquad \begin{array}{r} 94 \\ \times\ 7 \\ \hline \end{array} \qquad \begin{array}{r} 53 \\ \times\ 8 \\ \hline \end{array} \qquad \begin{array}{r} 58 \\ \times\ 4 \\ \hline \end{array}$$

3.
$$\begin{array}{r} 69 \\ \times\ 7 \\ \hline \end{array} \qquad \begin{array}{r} 28 \\ \times\ 4 \\ \hline \end{array} \qquad \begin{array}{r} 54 \\ \times\ 8 \\ \hline \end{array} \qquad \begin{array}{r} 57 \\ \times\ 8 \\ \hline \end{array} \qquad \begin{array}{r} 43 \\ \times\ 6 \\ \hline \end{array} \qquad \begin{array}{r} 33 \\ \times\ 9 \\ \hline \end{array} \qquad \begin{array}{r} 77 \\ \times\ 8 \\ \hline \end{array}$$

4.
$$\begin{array}{r} 42 \\ \times\ 7 \\ \hline \end{array} \qquad \begin{array}{r} 62 \\ \times\ 9 \\ \hline \end{array} \qquad \begin{array}{r} 18 \\ \times\ 4 \\ \hline \end{array} \qquad \begin{array}{r} 22 \\ \times\ 6 \\ \hline \end{array} \qquad \begin{array}{r} 29 \\ \times\ 7 \\ \hline \end{array} \qquad \begin{array}{r} 42 \\ \times\ 6 \\ \hline \end{array} \qquad \begin{array}{r} 53 \\ \times\ 5 \\ \hline \end{array}$$

5.
$$\begin{array}{r} 37 \\ \times\ 5 \\ \hline \end{array} \qquad \begin{array}{r} 96 \\ \times\ 3 \\ \hline \end{array} \qquad \begin{array}{r} 76 \\ \times\ 5 \\ \hline \end{array} \qquad \begin{array}{r} 65 \\ \times\ 4 \\ \hline \end{array} \qquad \begin{array}{r} 28 \\ \times\ 6 \\ \hline \end{array} \qquad \begin{array}{r} 77 \\ \times\ 6 \\ \hline \end{array} \qquad \begin{array}{r} 82 \\ \times\ 9 \\ \hline \end{array}$$

6.
$$\begin{array}{r} 33 \\ \times\ 8 \\ \hline \end{array} \qquad \begin{array}{r} 37 \\ \times\ 9 \\ \hline \end{array} \qquad \begin{array}{r} 26 \\ \times\ 7 \\ \hline \end{array} \qquad \begin{array}{r} 17 \\ \times\ 9 \\ \hline \end{array} \qquad \begin{array}{r} 24 \\ \times\ 8 \\ \hline \end{array} \qquad \begin{array}{r} 77 \\ \times\ 2 \\ \hline \end{array} \qquad \begin{array}{r} 54 \\ \times\ 6 \\ \hline \end{array}$$

Math Connection—Grade 3—RBP3799   www.summerbridgeactivities.com   © RBP Books

2-Digit Multiplication Practice

Solve each problem.

1.
   63   65   69   64   67   62   68
  x 7   x 3   x 5   x 9   x 7   x 8   x 4

2.
   77   71   70   75   76   79   74
  x 5   x 9   x 6   x 8   x 4   x 7   x 9

3.
   82   85   89   83   88   86   80
  x 7   x 6   x 3   x 9   x 5   x 7   x 8

4.
   90   92   96   95   99   94   98
  x 7   x 9   x 8   x 6   x 4   x 5   x 6

5.
   17   19   23   46   37   59   63
  x 7   x 7   x 7   x 7   x 7   x 7   x 7

6.
   63   21   92   83   47   76   58
  x 8   x 8   x 8   x 8   x 8   x 8   x 8

7.
   84   27   90   57   75   66   38
  x 9   x 9   x 9   x 9   x 9   x 9   x 9

2-Digit Multiplication Practice

Solve each problem.

1.

12	25	34	40	52	10	27
x 4	x 3	x 4	x 6	x 7	x 6	x 5

2.

36	45	57	15	21	39	46
x 3	x 3	x 4	x 3	x 9	x 5	x 7

3.

55	13	23	33	48	59	11
x 8	x 6	x 8	x 4	x 5	x 3	x 5

4.

28	37	42	53	14	20	35
x 4	x 6	x 9	x 9	x 7	x 5	x 2

5.

44	58	16	29	36	47	57
x 8	x 6	x 4	x 3	x 8	x 7	x 5

6.

18	26	38	49	56	35	32
x 4	x 6	x 7	x 4	x 7	x 8	x 9

Math Connection—Grade 3—RBP3799   www.summerbridgeactivities.com   © RBP Books

2-Digit Multiplication Problem Solving

Solve the problems. Do your work in the box. Write your answer on the line.

1. Jimmy wanted to bring cookies to school to share with his classmates.

He wanted each student to get 3 cookies. He has 29 students in his class.

How many cookies does he need to bring?

_____

2. Kara has 7 feet of ribbon.

She knows there are 12 inches in each foot.

How many inches of ribbon does she have?

_____

3. Tina rode her bike 17 miles each day for 6 days.

How many miles did Tina ride?

_____

4. Jack read 7 books.

Each book had 48 pages.

How many pages did Jack read?

_____

5. Marissa has 5 trading card books.

Each book has 50 cards in it.

How many trading cards does Marissa have?

_____

6. Juan put his stamp collection into 4 boxes.

He put 73 stamps in each box.

How many stamps does he have?

_____

2-Digit Multiplication Assessment

Solve each problem.

> Knowing your multiplication facts makes multiplying big numbers easy!

1.
$$\begin{array}{r} 26 \\ \times\ 10 \\ \hline \end{array} \qquad \begin{array}{r} 75 \\ \times\ 10 \\ \hline \end{array} \qquad \begin{array}{r} 83 \\ \times\ 10 \\ \hline \end{array} \qquad \begin{array}{r} 37 \\ \times\ 10 \\ \hline \end{array} \qquad \begin{array}{r} 54 \\ \times\ 10 \\ \hline \end{array}$$

2.
$$\begin{array}{r} 33 \\ \times\ 2 \\ \hline \end{array} \qquad \begin{array}{r} 42 \\ \times\ 2 \\ \hline \end{array} \qquad \begin{array}{r} 34 \\ \times\ 2 \\ \hline \end{array} \qquad \begin{array}{r} 14 \\ \times\ 2 \\ \hline \end{array} \qquad \begin{array}{r} 22 \\ \times\ 3 \\ \hline \end{array}$$

3.
$$\begin{array}{r} 47 \\ \times\ 4 \\ \hline \end{array} \qquad \begin{array}{r} 53 \\ \times\ 5 \\ \hline \end{array} \qquad \begin{array}{r} 62 \\ \times\ 7 \\ \hline \end{array} \qquad \begin{array}{r} 81 \\ \times\ 9 \\ \hline \end{array} \qquad \begin{array}{r} 37 \\ \times\ 6 \\ \hline \end{array}$$

4.
$$\begin{array}{r} 54 \\ \times\ 8 \\ \hline \end{array} \qquad \begin{array}{r} 77 \\ \times\ 9 \\ \hline \end{array} \qquad \begin{array}{r} 42 \\ \times\ 8 \\ \hline \end{array} \qquad \begin{array}{r} 68 \\ \times\ 4 \\ \hline \end{array} \qquad \begin{array}{r} 87 \\ \times\ 5 \\ \hline \end{array}$$

Solve the problem. Do your work in the box. Write your answer on the line.

5. During practice Josh ran four 75-meter sprints.

How many meters did Josh run?

_____

6. Hayden ran for 3 touchdowns. He ran 37 yards each run.

How many yards did Hayden run?

_____

Math Connection—Grade 3—RBP3799   www.summerbridgeactivities.com   © RBP Books

2-Digit Multiplication Assessment

Solve each problem.

1.

46	63	49	92	38
x 10	x 10	x 10	x 10	x 10

2.

31	41	43	13	20
x 3	x 2	x 2	x 3	x 3

3.

66	73	39	27	55
x 8	x 9	x 4	x 5	x 6

4.

74	83	73	58	34
x 7	x 8	x 6	x 2	x 6

Solve the problem. Do your work in the box. Write your answer on the line.

5. Samantha practiced gymnastics for 2 hours 5 days a week for 12 weeks.

How many hours did she practice?

_____

6. Halley ran 6 miles 3 days a week and 3 miles 2 days a week.

How many miles did she run each week?

_____

Division with Remainders

Solve the problems. Do your work in the box. Write your answer on the line.

There are 11 cookies. There are 3 children.
How many cookies will each child get? __3__
How many cookies are left over? __2__

Each child can have **3** cookies.
There are **2** cookies left over.

1. There are 14 pieces of paper. Miss Scriber wants them in 3 equal stacks.

   How many papers are in each stack? _____

   How many are left over? _____

2. Mark has 15 books. He put them on 2 shelves, with the same number of books on each shelf.

   How many books are on each shelf? _____

   How many books are left over? _____

3. Cal has 12 dog bones. He has 5 dogs.

   How many dog bones will each dog get?

   _____

   How many dog bones will be left over? _____

4. Jenny has 19 walnuts. She wants to divide them evenly between 3 bags.

   How many walnuts will be in each bag? _____

   How many walnuts will be left over? _____

5. Alex has 11 apples. He needs 5 apples to make a pie.

   How many pies can he make? _____

   How many apples will be left over? _____

6. Mother bought 15 cookies for dessert. There are 4 people in our family.

   How many cookies will each person get? _____

   How many cookies will be left over? _____

Division with Remainders

Solve each problem.

> Here is the way to divide.
>
> Divisor → 3)19 ← Dividend
>
> 1. Think. How many times will 3 go into 19? 3 x 6 = 18.
> 2. Then subtract. What is left is the remainder.
>
> $$\begin{array}{r} 6\,\text{r}1 \\ 3\overline{)19} \\ -18 \\ \hline 1 \end{array}$$

1. $2\overline{)15}$ $3\overline{)17}$ $4\overline{)19}$ $6\overline{)22}$

2. $4\overline{)25}$ $5\overline{)18}$ $7\overline{)23}$ $8\overline{)43}$

3. $9\overline{)70}$ $2\overline{)19}$ $4\overline{)21}$ $5\overline{)24}$

4. $7\overline{)30}$ $6\overline{)13}$ $8\overline{)25}$ $5\overline{)32}$

5. $4\overline{)17}$ $7\overline{)25}$ $9\overline{)42}$ $8\overline{)38}$

6. $5\overline{)19}$ $7\overline{)18}$ $8\overline{)17}$ $6\overline{)32}$

2-Digit Division with Remainders

Solve each problem.

---

1. See how many times the divisor will go into the tens.
   2 will go into the 3 one time. 1 x 2 = 2. Subtract. 3 − 2 = 1.
2. Then bring down the ones. 2 will go into 11 five times.
   2 x 5 = 10. There is a remainder of 1.

$$
\begin{array}{r}
\mathbf{15}\,\text{r1} \\
2\overline{)31} \\
-\,2 \\
\hline
11 \\
-\,10 \\
\hline
1
\end{array}
$$

---

1. $3\overline{)42}$ $4\overline{)54}$ $5\overline{)62}$ $2\overline{)43}$

2. $6\overline{)72}$ $8\overline{)92}$ $5\overline{)75}$ $4\overline{)62}$

3. $3\overline{)57}$ $2\overline{)42}$ $4\overline{)74}$ $5\overline{)81}$

4. $6\overline{)85}$ $7\overline{)83}$ $8\overline{)89}$ $7\overline{)80}$

5. $3\overline{)76}$ $4\overline{)59}$ $5\overline{)72}$ $3\overline{)48}$

Math Connection—Grade 3—RBP3799   www.summerbridgeactivities.com   © RBP Books

Division Practice

Solve each problem.

1. $3\overline{)9}$ $4\overline{)12}$ $5\overline{)15}$ $7\overline{)28}$ $8\overline{)32}$

2. $9\overline{)72}$ $5\overline{)35}$ $6\overline{)42}$ $8\overline{)64}$ $7\overline{)49}$

3. $3\overline{)19}$ $4\overline{)15}$ $5\overline{)18}$ $7\overline{)22}$ $9\overline{)29}$

4. $6\overline{)37}$ $7\overline{)39}$ $8\overline{)25}$ $5\overline{)27}$ $4\overline{)34}$

5. $5\overline{)55}$ $2\overline{)26}$ $3\overline{)39}$ $6\overline{)66}$ $4\overline{)48}$

6. $7\overline{)92}$ $8\overline{)97}$ $6\overline{)73}$ $5\overline{)86}$ $4\overline{)79}$

© RBP Books   www.summerbridgeactivities.com   Math Connection—Grade 3—RBP3799

Division Practice

Solve each problem.

> If you know your multiplication facts, dividing is a snap!

1. $6\overline{)23}$ $\qquad$ $8\overline{)38}$ $\qquad$ $5\overline{)43}$ $\qquad$ $6\overline{)52}$ $\qquad$ $8\overline{)63}$

2. $6\overline{)21}$ $\qquad$ $9\overline{)32}$ $\qquad$ $7\overline{)51}$ $\qquad$ $9\overline{)68}$ $\qquad$ $8\overline{)74}$

3. $8\overline{)37}$ $\qquad$ $5\overline{)46}$ $\qquad$ $8\overline{)42}$ $\qquad$ $7\overline{)65}$ $\qquad$ $9\overline{)76}$

4. $4\overline{)76}$ $\qquad$ $2\overline{)35}$ $\qquad$ $3\overline{)56}$ $\qquad$ $5\overline{)71}$ $\qquad$ $3\overline{)47}$

5. $5\overline{)62}$ $\qquad$ $3\overline{)84}$ $\qquad$ $3\overline{)78}$ $\qquad$ $2\overline{)44}$ $\qquad$ $3\overline{)67}$

6. $5\overline{)66}$ $\qquad$ $7\overline{)93}$ $\qquad$ $3\overline{)89}$ $\qquad$ $4\overline{)77}$ $\qquad$ $2\overline{)49}$

Division Assessment

Solve each problem.

1. $6\overline{)42}$ $7\overline{)56}$ $8\overline{)48}$ $9\overline{)63}$ $8\overline{)72}$

2. $3\overline{)66}$ $2\overline{)82}$ $5\overline{)95}$ $4\overline{)92}$ $6\overline{)96}$

3. $3\overline{)58}$ $4\overline{)47}$ $5\overline{)83}$ $7\overline{)94}$ $3\overline{)65}$

4. $5\overline{)78}$ $3\overline{)88}$ $7\overline{)72}$ $4\overline{)59}$ $3\overline{)83}$

Solve the problem. Write your answer on the line.

5. Jacob had 6 dogs.

He had a box of 47 dog biscuits.

How many biscuits does each dog get if Jacob gives each the same number?

How many biscuits are left over?

_____

6. Jana's coach wanted her to run 25 miles each week.

If she runs the same number of miles on 5 days, how many miles will she have to run each day?

_____

Division Assessment
Solve each problem.

1. $6\overline{)54}$ $7\overline{)49}$ $8\overline{)32}$ $9\overline{)72}$ $4\overline{)20}$

2. $3\overline{)63}$ $2\overline{)46}$ $5\overline{)85}$ $4\overline{)52}$ $6\overline{)72}$

3. $3\overline{)47}$ $4\overline{)59}$ $5\overline{)72}$ $7\overline{)99}$ $3\overline{)97}$

4. $5\overline{)88}$ $3\overline{)98}$ $7\overline{)92}$ $4\overline{)79}$ $3\overline{)73}$

Solve the problem. Write your answer on the line.

5. Cayden's piano teacher wants him to practice 12 hours each week.

If he practices the same amount of time each day for 6 days, how many hours will he practice each day?

6. Alex has 8 chicken coops.

He has 96 chickens.

How many chickens will be in each coop if he places the same number in each coop?

Geometry

Look at the geometric shapes. Answer the questions.

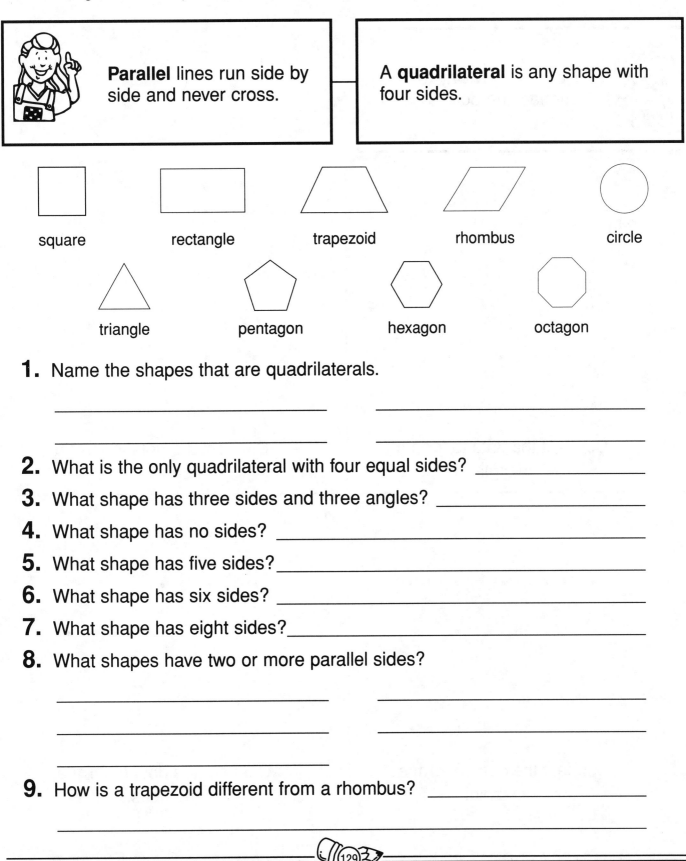

1. Name the shapes that are quadrilaterals.

   _____   _____

   _____   _____

2. What is the only quadrilateral with four equal sides? _____

3. What shape has three sides and three angles? _____

4. What shape has no sides? _____

5. What shape has five sides? _____

6. What shape has six sides? _____

7. What shape has eight sides? _____

8. What shapes have two or more parallel sides?

   _____   _____

   _____   _____

   _____

9. How is a trapezoid different from a rhombus? _____

Forming Geometric Shapes

Connect the dots to form different geometric shapes.

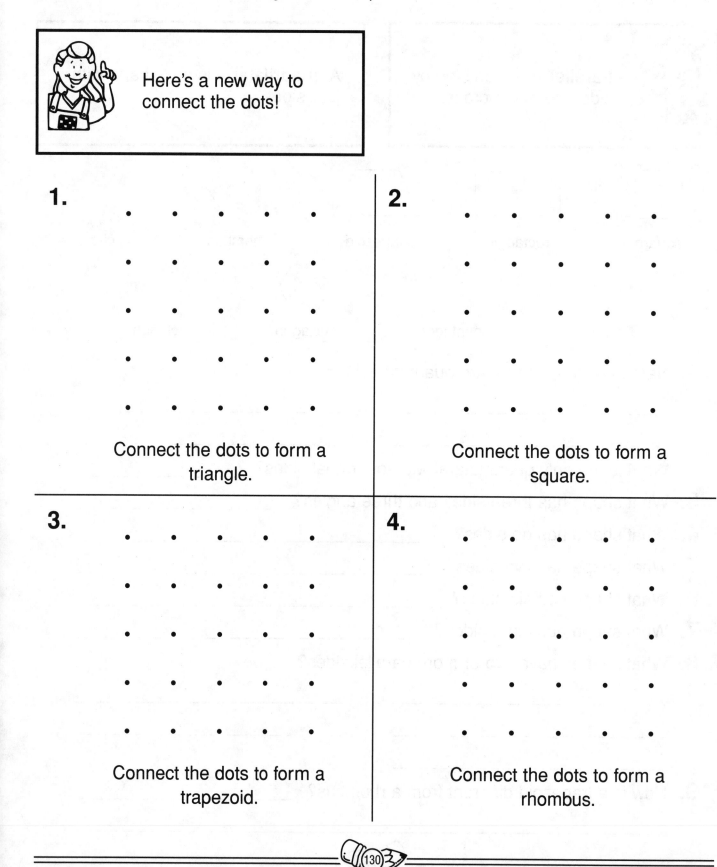

Here's a new way to connect the dots!

1.

Connect the dots to form a triangle.

2.

Connect the dots to form a square.

3.

Connect the dots to form a trapezoid.

4.

Connect the dots to form a rhombus.

Math Connection—Grade 3—RBP3799   www.summerbridgeactivities.com   © RBP Books

Exploring Symmetry

Tell whether each shape is divided symmetrically. Circle the correct answer.

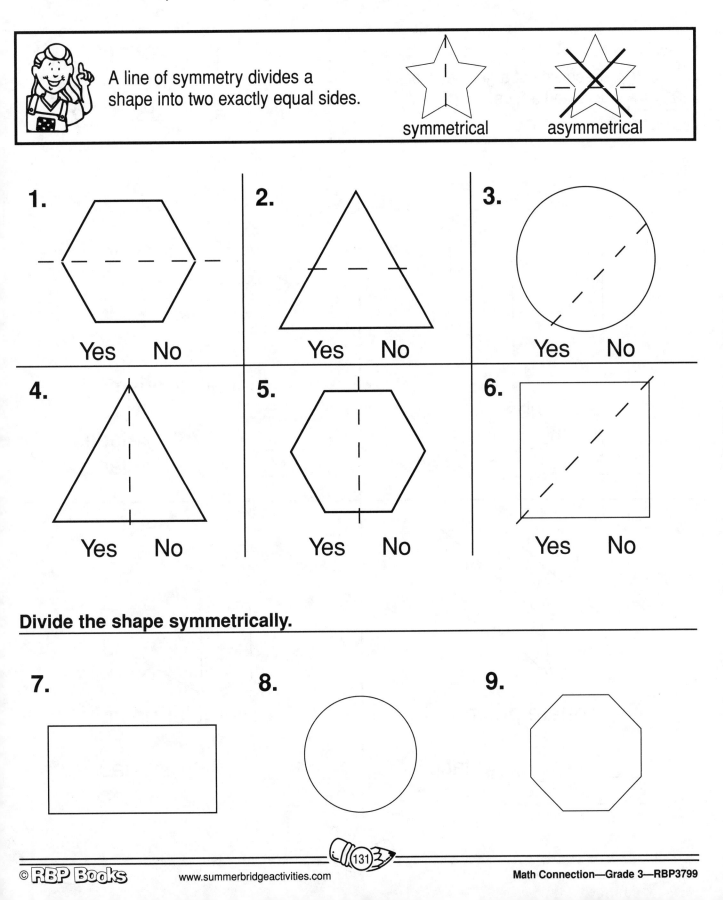

A line of symmetry divides a shape into two exactly equal sides.

symmetrical   asymmetrical

1. Yes   No

2. Yes   No

3. Yes   No

4. Yes   No

5. Yes   No

6. Yes   No

Divide the shape symmetrically.

7.

8.

9.

Exploring Geometric Solids

Look at the geometric solids. Write the number of faces each block has.

Each side of a geometric solid is called a **face**.

COOL! It's math in 3-D!

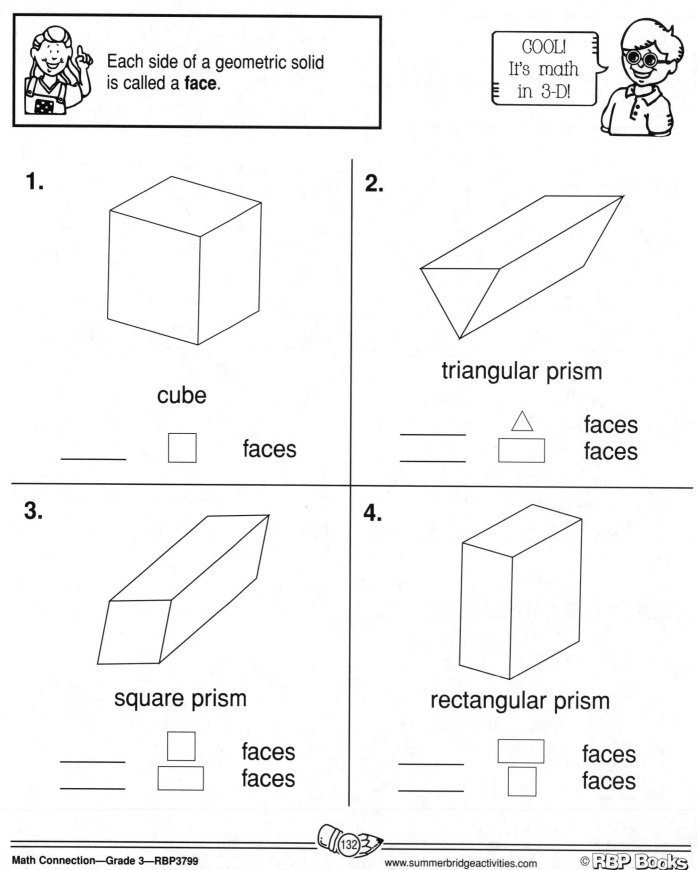

1.

cube

_____ ☐ faces

2.

triangular prism

_____ △ faces
_____ ☐ faces

3.

square prism

_____ ☐ faces
_____ ☐ faces

4.

rectangular prism

_____ ☐ faces
_____ ☐ faces

Fractions

Write the correct fraction.

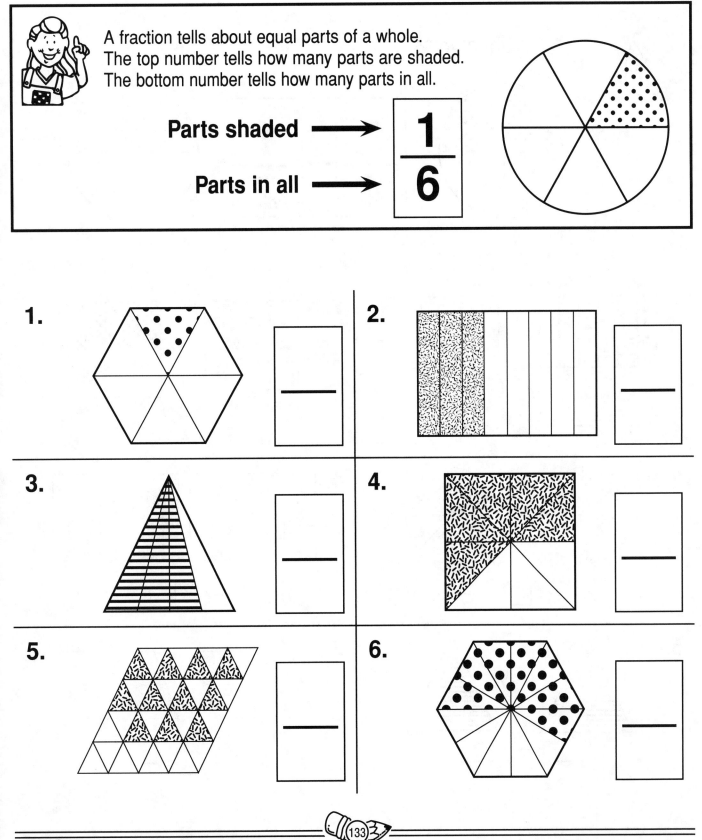

A fraction tells about equal parts of a whole.
The top number tells how many parts are shaded.
The bottom number tells how many parts in all.

Parts shaded ———→ $\dfrac{1}{6}$

Parts in all ———→

1.

2.

3.

4.

5.

6.

www.summerbridgeactivities.com   **Math Connection—Grade 3—RBP3799**

Fractions

Write the fractions; then use >, <, or = to compare the fractions.

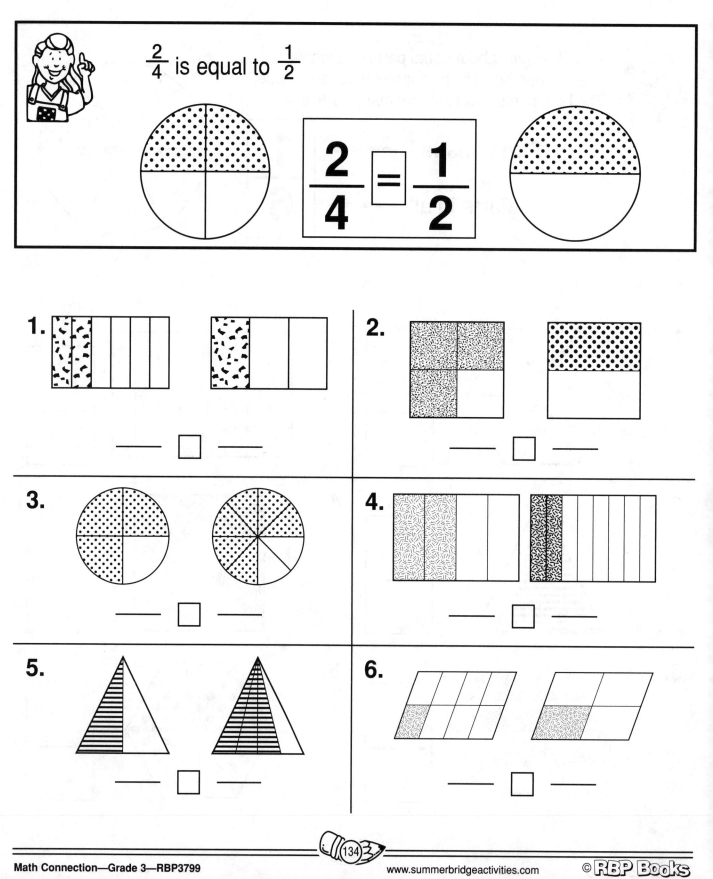

Equivalent Fractions

Fill in the missing numerals to show equivalent fractions.

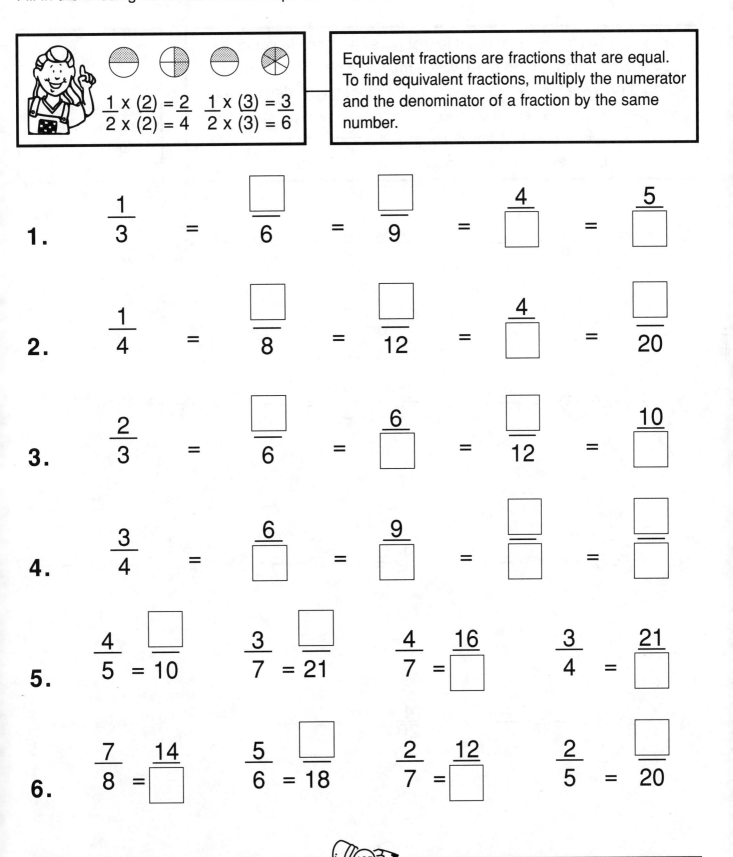

Equivalent fractions are fractions that are equal. To find equivalent fractions, multiply the numerator and the denominator of a fraction by the same number.

$\dfrac{1 \times (2)}{2 \times (2)} = \dfrac{2}{4}$ $\dfrac{1 \times (3)}{2 \times (3)} = \dfrac{3}{6}$

1. $\dfrac{1}{3} = \dfrac{\square}{6} = \dfrac{\square}{9} = \dfrac{4}{\square} = \dfrac{5}{\square}$

2. $\dfrac{1}{4} = \dfrac{\square}{8} = \dfrac{\square}{12} = \dfrac{4}{\square} = \dfrac{\square}{20}$

3. $\dfrac{2}{3} = \dfrac{\square}{6} = \dfrac{6}{\square} = \dfrac{\square}{12} = \dfrac{10}{\square}$

4. $\dfrac{3}{4} = \dfrac{6}{\square} = \dfrac{9}{\square} = \dfrac{\square}{\square} = \dfrac{\square}{\square}$

5. $\dfrac{4}{5} = \dfrac{\square}{10}$ $\dfrac{3}{7} = \dfrac{\square}{21}$ $\dfrac{4}{7} = \dfrac{16}{\square}$ $\dfrac{3}{4} = \dfrac{21}{\square}$

6. $\dfrac{7}{8} = \dfrac{14}{\square}$ $\dfrac{5}{6} = \dfrac{\square}{18}$ $\dfrac{2}{7} = \dfrac{12}{\square}$ $\dfrac{2}{5} = \dfrac{\square}{20}$

Reducing Fractions

Rename each fraction to its lowest term.

The <u>lowest term</u> is the lowest possible denominator for a fraction. To find the lowest term, find a number that you can divide evenly into both the numerator and the denominator. For $\frac{3}{6}$, 3 can be divided evenly in both 3 and 6, so $\frac{1}{2}$ is the lowest term for $\frac{3}{6}$.

$$\frac{3 \div (3)}{6 \div (3)} = \frac{1}{2}$$

Here's another place where knowing your basic facts really helps!

1. $\frac{4}{8} \div \frac{4}{4} =$ — $\frac{4}{12} \div \frac{4}{4} =$ — $\frac{5}{15} \div \frac{5}{5} =$ —

2. $\frac{4}{6} \div \frac{2}{2} =$ — $\frac{2}{12} \div \frac{2}{2} =$ — $\frac{3}{9} \div \frac{3}{3} =$ —

3. $\frac{3}{12} \div$ — $=$ — $\frac{4}{16} \div$ — $=$ — $\frac{3}{15} \div$ — $=$ —

4. $\frac{9}{63} \div$ — $=$ — $\frac{4}{20} \div$ — $=$ — $\frac{8}{24} \div$ — $=$ —

Math Connection—Grade 3—RBP3799   www.summerbridgeactivities.com   © RBP Books

Improper Fractions

Rewrite each fraction as a mixed number. Reduce each fraction to its lowest terms.

$\frac{5}{3}$ is called an improper fraction because the numerator is larger than the denominator. $\frac{3}{3}$ equals 1, so $\frac{5}{3}$ equals 1 and $\frac{2}{3}$. $1\frac{2}{3}$ is called a mixed number.

To change an improper fraction to a mixed number, divide the numerator by the denominator and place the remainder as the numerator. $\frac{13}{3} = 4\frac{1}{3}$, or $13 \div 3 = 4$ with 1 remaining.

1. $\frac{14}{3} =$ ___ $\frac{12}{5} =$ ___ $\frac{17}{4} =$ ___ $\frac{13}{2} =$ ___

2. $\frac{12}{7} =$ ___ $\frac{18}{5} =$ ___ $\frac{27}{4} =$ ___ $\frac{23}{5} =$ ___

3. $\frac{11}{3} =$ ___ $\frac{15}{4} =$ ___ $\frac{24}{5} =$ ___ $\frac{19}{3} =$ ___

4. $\frac{38}{4} =$ ___ $\frac{66}{8} =$ ___ $\frac{44}{6} =$ ___ $\frac{84}{9} =$ ___

5. $\frac{18}{8} =$ ___ $\frac{26}{6} =$ ___ $\frac{39}{6} =$ ___ $\frac{42}{8} =$ ___

Fraction Assessment

Write the fractions; then use >, <, or = to compare.

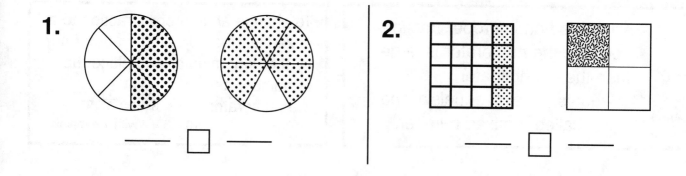

1. ⎯⎯ □ ⎯⎯

2. ⎯⎯ □ ⎯⎯

Cross out the fraction that is not equivalent to the first fraction.

3. $\frac{1}{3}$ = $\frac{2}{6}$ $\frac{3}{9}$ $\frac{4}{8}$ $\frac{5}{15}$ $\frac{6}{18}$

4. $\frac{1}{4}$ = $\frac{2}{8}$ $\frac{3}{6}$ $\frac{4}{16}$ $\frac{5}{20}$ $\frac{6}{24}$

Rename each fraction to its lowest term.

5. $\frac{4}{12}$ = ⎯⎯ $\frac{8}{16}$ = ⎯⎯ $\frac{5}{15}$ = ⎯⎯ $\frac{6}{18}$ = ⎯⎯

Rename each fraction as a mixed number.

6. $\frac{17}{3}$ = ⎯⎯ $\frac{13}{5}$ = ⎯⎯ $\frac{44}{8}$ = ⎯⎯ $\frac{28}{6}$ = ⎯⎯

Fraction Assessment

Write the fractions; then use >, <, or = to compare.

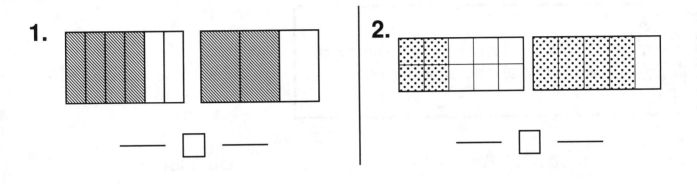

1. ___ — □ — ___

2. ___ — □ — ___

Cross out the fraction that is not equivalent to the first fraction.

3. $\dfrac{1}{5}$ = $\dfrac{2}{6}$ $\dfrac{2}{10}$ $\dfrac{3}{15}$ $\dfrac{4}{20}$ $\dfrac{5}{25}$

4. $\dfrac{2}{3}$ = $\dfrac{4}{6}$ $\dfrac{6}{9}$ $\dfrac{8}{16}$ $\dfrac{10}{15}$ $\dfrac{12}{18}$

Rename each fraction to its lowest term.

5. $\dfrac{9}{18}$ = ___ $\dfrac{8}{24}$ = ___ $\dfrac{8}{12}$ = ___ $\dfrac{15}{20}$ = ___

Rename each fraction as a mixed number.

6. $\dfrac{17}{5}$ = ___ $\dfrac{13}{6}$ = ___ $\dfrac{57}{9}$ = ___ $\dfrac{26}{8}$ = ___

Exploring Probability

Look at the spinners. Answer the questions.

To have equal chances, the colors must have an equal number of spaces.

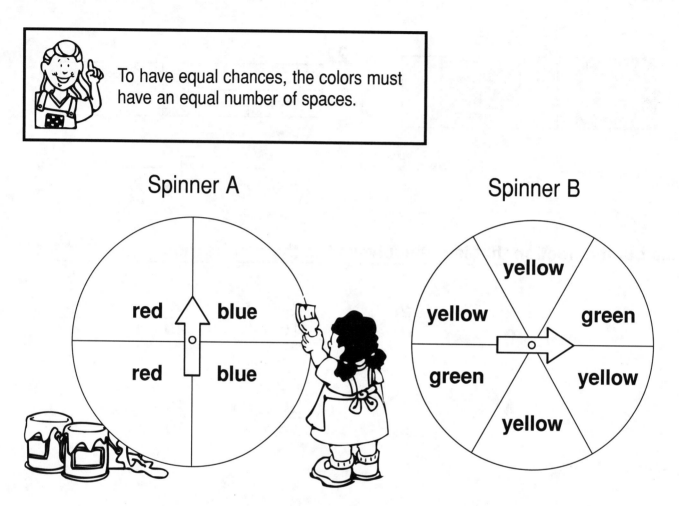

Spinner A

Spinner B

1. On Spinner A, would you have more chances of spinning red or blue, or would your chances be equal? _____

2. On Spinner B, would you have more chances of spinning yellow or green, or would your chances be equal? _____

3. What are the chances of spinning red on Spinner B? _____

4. On Spinner A, you have a 2 out of 4 chance of spinning either red or blue. On Spinner B, how many chances out of 6 do you have of spinning green?

   _____

5. On spinner B, how many chances out of 6 do you have of spinning yellow?

   _____

Math Connection—Grade 3—RBP3799   www.summerbridgeactivities.com   © RBP Books

Exploring Probability

Read the graph. Answer the questions.

We can get a lot of
information from a graph.

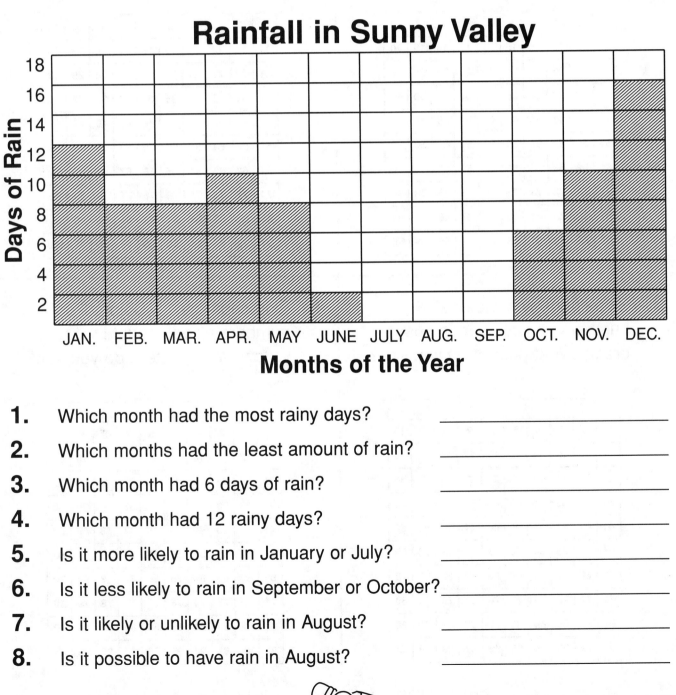

Rainfall in Sunny Valley

1. Which month had the most rainy days? _____

2. Which months had the least amount of rain? _____

3. Which month had 6 days of rain? _____

4. Which month had 12 rainy days? _____

5. Is it more likely to rain in January or July? _____

6. Is it less likely to rain in September or October? _____

7. Is it likely or unlikely to rain in August? _____

8. Is it possible to have rain in August? _____

www.summerbridgeactivities.com   Math Connection—Grade 3—RBP3799

Number Patterns
Follow the directions.

1. Skip count by 3. Color all the numbers as you count by 3s red. What pattern do you see?

1	2	3	4	5	6	7	8	9	10
11	12	13	14	15	16	17	18	19	20
21	22	23	24	25	26	27	28	29	30
31	32	33	34	35	36	37	38	39	40
41	42	43	44	45	46	47	48	49	50
51	52	53	54	55	56	57	58	59	60
61	62	63	64	65	66	67	68	69	70
71	72	73	74	75	76	77	78	79	80
81	82	83	84	85	86	87	88	89	90
91	92	93	94	95	96	97	98	99	100

2. Skip count by 4. Color all the numbers as you count by 4s blue. What pattern do you see?

1	2	3	4	5	6	7	8	9	10
11	12	13	14	15	16	17	18	19	20
21	22	23	24	25	26	27	28	29	30
31	32	33	34	35	36	37	38	39	40
41	42	43	44	45	46	47	48	49	50
51	52	53	54	55	56	57	58	59	60
61	62	63	64	65	66	67	68	69	70
71	72	73	74	75	76	77	78	79	80
81	82	83	84	85	86	87	88	89	90
91	92	93	94	95	96	97	98	99	100

3. Skip count by 6. Color all the numbers as you count by 6s green. What pattern do you see?

1	2	3	4	5	6	7	8	9	10
11	12	13	14	15	16	17	18	19	20
21	22	23	24	25	26	27	28	29	30
31	32	33	34	35	36	37	38	39	40
41	42	43	44	45	46	47	48	49	50
51	52	53	54	55	56	57	58	59	60
61	62	63	64	65	66	67	68	69	70
71	72	73	74	75	76	77	78	79	80
81	82	83	84	85	86	87	88	89	90
91	92	93	94	95	96	97	98	99	100

4. Skip count by 11. Color all the numbers as you count by 11s yellow. What pattern do you see?

1	2	3	4	5	6	7	8	9	10
11	12	13	14	15	16	17	18	19	20
21	22	23	24	25	26	27	28	29	30
31	32	33	34	35	36	37	38	39	40
41	42	43	44	45	46	47	48	49	50
51	52	53	54	55	56	57	58	59	60
61	62	63	64	65	66	67	68	69	70
71	72	73	74	75	76	77	78	79	80
81	82	83	84	85	86	87	88	89	90
91	92	93	94	95	96	97	98	99	100

Patterns and Functions

Look at the patterns. Fill in the charts.

	Patterns are cool. They go on forever!		Finding patterns is helpful in solving problems.

1.

Rule: [ ] x 2 + 1	
2	5
3	7
4	9
5	11
6	
7	
8	

2.

Rule: [ ] x 3 – 2	
2	4
3	7
4	10
5	
6	
7	
8	

3.

Rule: [ ] x 5 + 1	
2	11
3	16
4	21
5	
6	
7	
8	

4.

Rule: [ ] – 2 x 4	
2	0
3	4
4	8
5	
6	
7	
8	

What's the rule?

5.

Rule:	
2	8
3	11
4	14
5	17
6	20
7	23
8	26

6.

Rule:	
2	0
3	3
4	6
5	9
6	12
7	15
8	18

www.summerbridgeactivities.com   **Math Connection—Grade 3—RBP3799**

Pre-Algebra

Solve the problems.

◆ and ● are **variables**. Variables stand for numbers.
If ◆ is equal to 2, then ● must be equal to 6.

$$\blacklozenge + \bullet = 8$$

Here is another place that knowing your basic facts helps you do harder math.

1.

▼ + ★ = 13

If ▼ is 1, then ★ is _____**12**_____

If ▼ is 6, then ★ is _____

If ▼ is 9, then ★ is _____

If ★ is 5, then ▼ is _____

2.

♣ − ■ = 6

If ♣ is 9, then ■ is _____

If ♣ is 14, then ■ is _____

If ■ is 7, then ♣ is _____

If ■ is 11, then ♣ is _____

3.

❖ × ♠ = 24

If ❖ is 12, then ♠ is _____

If ❖ is 6, then ♠ is _____

If ♠ is 3, then ❖ is _____

If ♠ is 8, then ❖ is _____

4.

✺ × ❄ = 48

If ✺ is 6, then ❄ is _____

If ✺ is 4, then ❄ is _____

If ❄ is 3, then ✺ is _____

If ❄ is 12, then ✺ is _____

Addition Review

Solve each problem.

1.

$$7 + 6 \qquad 9 + 8 \qquad 5 + 7 \qquad 3 + 9 \qquad 4 + 8 \qquad 6 + 5 \qquad 10 + 3$$

2.

$$13 + 26 \qquad 46 + 30 \qquad 25 + 40 \qquad 74 + 12 \qquad 32 + 53 \qquad 60 + 28 \qquad 91 + 4$$

3.

$$4 + 3 + 2 \qquad 5 + 5 + 3 \qquad 8 + 5 + 5 \qquad 6 + 3 + 4 \qquad 7 + 1 + 5 \qquad 3 + 4 + 9 \qquad 1 + 7 + 5$$

4.

$$27 + 93 \qquad 46 + 72 \qquad 95 + 38 \qquad 32 + 87 \qquad 59 + 25 \qquad 76 + 28 \qquad 84 + 39$$

5.

$$67 + 99 \qquad 431 + 577 \qquad 297 + 329 \qquad 375 + 476 \qquad 596 + 627 \qquad 722 + 188 \qquad 830 + 275$$

6.

$$9{,}432 + 4{,}588 \qquad 7{,}657 + 3{,}579 \qquad 3{,}804 + 4{,}577 \qquad 5{,}931 + 3{,}999 \qquad 8{,}615 + 2{,}086 \qquad 2{,}793 + 9{,}558$$

     www.summerbridgeactivities.com   **Math Connection—Grade 3—RBP3799**

Subtraction Review

Solve each problem.

1.
$$
\begin{array}{r} 9 \\ -3 \\ \hline \end{array}
\quad
\begin{array}{r} 7 \\ -2 \\ \hline \end{array}
\quad
\begin{array}{r} 6 \\ -3 \\ \hline \end{array}
\quad
\begin{array}{r} 8 \\ -6 \\ \hline \end{array}
\quad
\begin{array}{r} 9 \\ -5 \\ \hline \end{array}
\quad
\begin{array}{r} 5 \\ -2 \\ \hline \end{array}
\quad
\begin{array}{r} 7 \\ -4 \\ \hline \end{array}
$$

2.
$$
\begin{array}{r} 53 \\ -12 \\ \hline \end{array}
\quad
\begin{array}{r} 94 \\ -43 \\ \hline \end{array}
\quad
\begin{array}{r} 46 \\ -24 \\ \hline \end{array}
\quad
\begin{array}{r} 85 \\ -33 \\ \hline \end{array}
\quad
\begin{array}{r} 77 \\ -52 \\ \hline \end{array}
\quad
\begin{array}{r} 69 \\ -36 \\ \hline \end{array}
\quad
\begin{array}{r} 88 \\ -46 \\ \hline \end{array}
$$

3.
$$
\begin{array}{r} 92 \\ -26 \\ \hline \end{array}
\quad
\begin{array}{r} 76 \\ -47 \\ \hline \end{array}
\quad
\begin{array}{r} 54 \\ -28 \\ \hline \end{array}
\quad
\begin{array}{r} 90 \\ -59 \\ \hline \end{array}
\quad
\begin{array}{r} 63 \\ -28 \\ \hline \end{array}
\quad
\begin{array}{r} 82 \\ -37 \\ \hline \end{array}
\quad
\begin{array}{r} 58 \\ -18 \\ \hline \end{array}
$$

4.
$$
\begin{array}{r} 943 \\ -263 \\ \hline \end{array}
\quad
\begin{array}{r} 745 \\ -238 \\ \hline \end{array}
\quad
\begin{array}{r} 876 \\ -294 \\ \hline \end{array}
\quad
\begin{array}{r} 833 \\ -550 \\ \hline \end{array}
\quad
\begin{array}{r} 904 \\ -308 \\ \hline \end{array}
\quad
\begin{array}{r} 730 \\ -423 \\ \hline \end{array}
\quad
\begin{array}{r} 500 \\ -275 \\ \hline \end{array}
$$

5.
$$
\begin{array}{r} 960 \\ -483 \\ \hline \end{array}
\quad
\begin{array}{r} 459 \\ -179 \\ \hline \end{array}
\quad
\begin{array}{r} 387 \\ -188 \\ \hline \end{array}
\quad
\begin{array}{r} 558 \\ -269 \\ \hline \end{array}
\quad
\begin{array}{r} 973 \\ -355 \\ \hline \end{array}
\quad
\begin{array}{r} 807 \\ -289 \\ \hline \end{array}
\quad
\begin{array}{r} 636 \\ -277 \\ \hline \end{array}
$$

6.
$$
\begin{array}{r} 8{,}467 \\ -4{,}435 \\ \hline \end{array}
\quad
\begin{array}{r} 3{,}956 \\ -1{,}846 \\ \hline \end{array}
\quad
\begin{array}{r} 7{,}578 \\ -2{,}357 \\ \hline \end{array}
\quad
\begin{array}{r} 9{,}475 \\ -1{,}275 \\ \hline \end{array}
\quad
\begin{array}{r} 6{,}375 \\ -4{,}161 \\ \hline \end{array}
\quad
\begin{array}{r} 5{,}687 \\ -1{,}453 \\ \hline \end{array}
$$

Math Connection—Grade 3—RBP3799   www.summerbridgeactivities.com   © RBP Books

Multiplication Review

Solve each problem.

1.
$$\begin{array}{r} 7 \\ \times\,2 \\ \hline \end{array} \qquad \begin{array}{r} 3 \\ \times\,5 \\ \hline \end{array} \qquad \begin{array}{r} 9 \\ \times\,3 \\ \hline \end{array} \qquad \begin{array}{r} 5 \\ \times\,4 \\ \hline \end{array} \qquad \begin{array}{r} 6 \\ \times\,2 \\ \hline \end{array} \qquad \begin{array}{r} 7 \\ \times\,5 \\ \hline \end{array} \qquad \begin{array}{r} 4 \\ \times\,6 \\ \hline \end{array}$$

2.
$$\begin{array}{r} 2 \\ \times\,5 \\ \hline \end{array} \qquad \begin{array}{r} 4 \\ \times\,7 \\ \hline \end{array} \qquad \begin{array}{r} 6 \\ \times\,9 \\ \hline \end{array} \qquad \begin{array}{r} 8 \\ \times\,7 \\ \hline \end{array} \qquad \begin{array}{r} 10 \\ \times\,4 \\ \hline \end{array} \qquad \begin{array}{r} 5 \\ \times\,9 \\ \hline \end{array} \qquad \begin{array}{r} 7 \\ \times\,8 \\ \hline \end{array}$$

3.
$$\begin{array}{r} 8 \\ \times\,9 \\ \hline \end{array} \qquad \begin{array}{r} 7 \\ \times\,9 \\ \hline \end{array} \qquad \begin{array}{r} 8 \\ \times\,8 \\ \hline \end{array} \qquad \begin{array}{r} 9 \\ \times\,9 \\ \hline \end{array} \qquad \begin{array}{r} 6 \\ \times\,7 \\ \hline \end{array} \qquad \begin{array}{r} 9 \\ \times\,8 \\ \hline \end{array} \qquad \begin{array}{r} 9 \\ \times\,5 \\ \hline \end{array}$$

4.
$$\begin{array}{r} 30 \\ \times\,3 \\ \hline \end{array} \qquad \begin{array}{r} 50 \\ \times\,7 \\ \hline \end{array} \qquad \begin{array}{r} 20 \\ \times\,6 \\ \hline \end{array} \qquad \begin{array}{r} 20 \\ \times\,4 \\ \hline \end{array} \qquad \begin{array}{r} 60 \\ \times\,9 \\ \hline \end{array} \qquad \begin{array}{r} 40 \\ \times\,8 \\ \hline \end{array} \qquad \begin{array}{r} 70 \\ \times\,7 \\ \hline \end{array}$$

5.
$$\begin{array}{r} 44 \\ \times\,3 \\ \hline \end{array} \qquad \begin{array}{r} 37 \\ \times\,4 \\ \hline \end{array} \qquad \begin{array}{r} 29 \\ \times\,3 \\ \hline \end{array} \qquad \begin{array}{r} 45 \\ \times\,2 \\ \hline \end{array} \qquad \begin{array}{r} 93 \\ \times\,8 \\ \hline \end{array} \qquad \begin{array}{r} 58 \\ \times\,7 \\ \hline \end{array} \qquad \begin{array}{r} 32 \\ \times\,6 \\ \hline \end{array}$$

6.
$$\begin{array}{r} 13 \\ \times\,7 \\ \hline \end{array} \qquad \begin{array}{r} 43 \\ \times\,8 \\ \hline \end{array} \qquad \begin{array}{r} 82 \\ \times\,4 \\ \hline \end{array} \qquad \begin{array}{r} 28 \\ \times\,3 \\ \hline \end{array} \qquad \begin{array}{r} 93 \\ \times\,6 \\ \hline \end{array} \qquad \begin{array}{r} 87 \\ \times\,9 \\ \hline \end{array} \qquad \begin{array}{r} 85 \\ \times\,4 \\ \hline \end{array}$$

Division Review

Solve each problem.

1. $8 \div 4 =$ ___ $18 \div 3 =$ ___ $16 \div 2 =$ ___ $14 \div 2 =$ ___

2. $5 \div 5 =$ ___ $20 \div 4 =$ ___ $27 \div 3 =$ ___ $28 \div 4 =$ ___

3. $35 \div 7 =$ ___ $63 \div 9 =$ ___ $56 \div 7 =$ ___ $36 \div 6 =$ ___

4. $64 \div 8 =$ ___ $54 \div 6 =$ ___ $32 \div 4 =$ ___ $35 \div 5 =$ ___

---

5. $5\overline{)45}$ $3\overline{)24}$ $3\overline{)21}$ $4\overline{)12}$ $4\overline{)16}$ $9\overline{)81}$

6. $8\overline{)72}$ $9\overline{)18}$ $7\overline{)49}$ $5\overline{)30}$ $8\overline{)48}$ $6\overline{)18}$

7. $6\overline{)38}$ $5\overline{)42}$ $7\overline{)46}$ $4\overline{)30}$ $8\overline{)67}$ $9\overline{)40}$

8.

(7 / 8 56)

___ x ___ = _____
___ x ___ = _____
___ ÷ ___ = _____
___ ÷ ___ = _____

9.

(6 / 7 42)

___ x ___ = _____
___ x ___ = _____
___ ÷ ___ = _____
___ ÷ ___ = _____

Math Connection—Grade 3—RBP3799

Name _____   Date _____

Mixed Review
Solve each problem.

1.

5	4	9	7	6	2	8
x 4	x 6	x 7	x 3	x 5	x 8	x 9

2. $3\overline{)27}$ $7\overline{)28}$ $6\overline{)42}$ $5\overline{)40}$ $8\overline{)64}$ $6\overline{)36}$

3. $81 \div 9 =$ ___ $7 \times 5 =$ ___ $28 \div 4 =$ ___ $2 \times 8 =$ ___

4. $6 \times 7 =$ ___ $24 \div 6 =$ ___ $18 \div 3 =$ ___ $7 \times 7 =$ ___

5. $8 \times 3 =$ ___ $27 \div 9 =$ ___ $20 \div 5 =$ ___ $6 \times 9 =$ ___

6. $10 \times 6 =$ ___ $54 \div 6 =$ ___ $8 \times 8 =$ ___ $48 \div 8 =$ ___

7.

275	437	769	840	653	693
+ 329	+392	+ 278	− 327	+ 354	− 185

8.

3	24	16	19		
9	13	34	43	550	853
+ 4	+17	+ 56	+ 21	+ 329	− 403

www.summerbridgeactivities.com   **Math Connection—Grade 3—RBP3799**

Answer Pages

Diagnostic Test 1—Page 4

1.	9	12	13	15	13	15
2.	4	7	6	4	6	7
3.	13	17	16	10	14	16
4.	1	4	6	7	9	11
	13	16	17	19		
5.	35	48	60	73	84	
6.	<	<	<	=	>	<
7.	8	12	20	35	41	59

Diagnostic Test 2—Page 5

1.	55	93	58	79	97	69
2.	12	12	11	26	32	63
3.	81	101	61	80	62	160
4.	15	13	34	56	13	39
5.	5:35	7:47	9:23	11:07		

9. **10.** **11.** **12.** (clock faces)

13. 43¢   **14.** 77¢   **15.** $7.80

Diagnostic Test 3—Page 6

1. 5 hundreds 6 tens 9 ones
2. 2 hundreds 9 tens 7 ones
3. 4 thousands 2 hundreds 0 tens 3 ones
4. 700   **5.** 80   **6.** 900   **7.** 3,000
8. > > > >

9.	579	999	776	659	972	885
10.	826	701	1,300	684	922	773
11.	221	442	510	223	221	310
12.	109	132	225	376	312	160

Diagnostic Test 4—Page 7

1.	15	8	24	35	56	27
2.	42	0	81	7	30	32
3.	6	3	6	8	6	4
4.	8	9	8	5	7	4
5.	70	180	340	230	780	990
6.	26	28	36	77	99	62
7.	75	238	272	260	656	222
8.	5r2	9r3	3r2	8r6	7r5	7r1
9.	18r2	16r3	18r1	11r5	13r2	14
10.	4 x 6 = 24	6 x 4 = 24	24 ÷ 6 = 4	24 ÷ 4 = 6		
11.	7 x 8 = 56	8 x 7 = 56	56 ÷ 7 = 8	56 ÷ 8 = 7		
12.	9 x 4 = 36	4 x 9 = 36	36 ÷ 4 = 9	36 ÷ 9 = 4		

Diagnostic Test 5—Page 8

1. 3 in.   **2.** 1 in.   **3.** 8 in.
4. 5 cm   **5.** 2 cm   **6.** $6\frac{1}{2}$ cm
7. **8.** **9.** (shapes)

10. cube
11. triangular prism
12. rectangular prism
13. $\frac{1}{4} < \frac{3}{4}$
14. $\frac{4}{8} > \frac{3}{8}$

Page 10

1.	6	1	3	10	7
2.	4	2	9	5	8
3.	13	12	20	18	40
4.	16	17	11	30	50
5.	64	31	72	27	81
6.	98	53	85	46	93

Page 11

0	1	2	3	4	5	6	7	8	9
10	11	12	13	14	15	16	17	18	19
20	21	22	23	24	25	26	27	28	29
30	31	32	33	34	35	36	37	38	39
40	41	42	43	44	45	46	47	48	49
50	51	52	53	54	55	56	57	58	59
60	61	62	63	64	65	66	67	68	69
70	71	72	73	74	75	76	77	78	79
80	81	82	83	84	85	86	87	88	89
90	91	92	93	94	95	96	97	98	99

Page 12

1.	32	26	50	36	42	10	48
2.	27	39	47	21	45	15	
3.	72	56	94	80	82	62	68
4.	67	59	85	73	91	55	89	75

Page 13

1. 6 tens 2 ones = 62   **2.** 4 tens 8 ones = 48
3. 2 tens 8 ones = 28   **4.** 1 ten 9 ones = 19
5. 7 tens 3 ones = 73   **6.** 3 tens 8 ones = 38
7. 4 tens 0 ones = 40   **8.** 8 tens 2 ones = 82
9. 5 tens 8 ones = 58

Page 14

1. >   **2.** >   **3.** <   **4.** =   **5.** <
6. >   **7.** <   **8.** <   **9.** =   **10.** <

Page 15

1. 1 hundred 5 tens 4 ones = 154
2. 1 hundred 6 tens 5 ones = 165
3. 2 hundreds 0 tens 7 ones = 207
4. 2 hundreds 8 tens 7 ones = 287
5. 3 hundreds 0 tens 8 ones = 308
6. 3 hundreds 3 tens 2 ones = 332
7. 3 hundreds 5 tens 1 one = 351
8. 2 hundreds 8 tens 3 ones = 283
9. 3 hundreds 0 tens 3 ones = 303

Page 16

1. f   **2.** c   **3.** e   **4.** g
5. h   **6.** a   **7.** d   **8.** b
9. 60   **10.** 700   **11.** 70   **12.** 9
13. 600   **14.** 900   **15.** 20

Page 17

1. c   **2.** g   **3.** d   **4.** h
5. i   **6.** j   **7.** e   **8.** a
9. f   **10.** b   **11.** 313   **12.** 809
13. 426   **14.** 211   **15.** 751   **16.** 105
17. 532   **18.** 944

Math Connection—Grade 3—RBP3799   www.summerbridgeactivities.com   © RBP Books

Answer Pages

Page 18
1. 149 2. 566 3. 430 4. 390
5. 804 6. 990 7. 709 8. 871
9. 990 10. 805
11. < 12. > 13. < 14. = 15. <
16. < 17. = 18. < 19. > 20. <

Page 19
1. <u>1</u> thousand <u>3</u> hundreds <u>4</u> tens <u>5</u> ones = 1,345
2. <u>2</u> thousands <u>1</u> hundred <u>6</u> tens <u>1</u> one = 2,161
3. <u>1</u> thousand <u>0</u> hundreds <u>3</u> tens <u>8</u> ones = 1,038
4. <u>3</u> thousands <u>1</u> hundred <u>0</u> tens <u>2</u> ones = 3,102
5. <u>2</u> thousands <u>4</u> hundreds <u>4</u> tens <u>0</u> ones = 2,440
6. <u>1</u> thousand <u>2</u> hundreds <u>1</u> ten <u>3</u> ones = 1,213

Page 20
1.	5,000	700	30	9
2.	4,000	600	50	0
3.	7,000	300	80	1
4.	0	700	30	6
5.	1,000	400	70	5
6.	5,000	800	30	7
7.	6,000	900	0	2
8.	4,000	500	60	0
9.	1,000	0	40	8
10.	1,000	100	10	1

11. 5 12. 3 13. 5 14. 2
15. 6 16. 2 17. 4 18. 7

Page 21
1. 1,533 2. 5,947 3. 3,755
4. 7,479 5. 9,021 6. 3,102
7. 3,506 8. 6,098 9. 3,609
10. 1,698
11. 3,000 + 400 + 50 + 6
12. 7,000 + 300 + 20 + 4
13. 9,000 + 100 + 50 + 2
14. 3,000 + 500 + 60 + 9
15. 2,000 + 400 + 30 + 1
16. 4,000 + 20 + 2

Page 22
1. four thousand twelve
2. four thousand seven hundred twenty
3. six thousand nine hundred ninety-nine
4. four thousand two hundred three
5. six thousand two
6. six thousand three hundred sixteen
7. 3,416 8. 9,350 9. 7,021
10. 1,592 11. 4,206 12. 9,999
13. three thousand three hundred ninety-six
14. four thousand five hundred fifty-three
15. eight thousand fifty-six
16. three thousand six hundred twenty-one
17. seven thousand two hundred fifty
18. three thousand three hundred two

Page 23
1. > 2. < 3. > 4. < 5. <
6. > 7. > 8. > 9. < 10. >
11. 49,377 51,790 52,763 70,459 73,210
12. 111,997 112,948 120,725 241,350 326,291
13. 7,205 6,249 5,927 3,463 2,944
14. 22,341 21,050 18,293 17,356 8,516

Page 24
1. twenty-seven
2. three hundred forty-six
3. fifty-nine
4. one hundred eight
5. nine thousand two hundred thirteen
6. 34 7. 516 8. 61 9. 780 10. 2,992
11. 200 12. 40 13. 7 14. > 15. <
16. < 17. > 18. < 19. >
20. 230, 429, 517, 610, 804
21. 7,391 7,382 7,380 7,378 7,197
22. 368 23. 4,215
23. 600 + 40 + 8 25. 1,000 + 500 + 20 + 9

Page 25
1. thirty-one
2. sixty-four
3. two hundred nineteen
4. five hundred seven
5. eight thousand three hundred ninety
6. 23 7. 452 8. 78 9. 687 10. 3,017
11. 30 12. 1 13. 5000 14. < 15. >
16. > 17. < 18. > 19. <
20. 379, 397, 739, 793, 937
21. 4,825 4,820 4,819 4,802 4,189
22. 596 23. 3,176
23. 900 + 2 25. 8000 + 800 + 20 + 1

Page 26
1.	4	9	9	8	10	12
2.	13	7	5	7	18	13
3.	9	8	16	13	15	6
4.	8	10	11	14	11	12
5.	12	15	10	11	16	10
6.	6	14	17	12	11	14

Page 27
1.	10	10	7	8	12	11
2.	6	9	17	8	7	12
3.	12	13	16	11	6	12
4.	9	14	13	13	16	15
5.	15	11	13	11	8	14
6.	18	16	10	13	17	15

Page 28
1.	6	7	9	10	11	11	12
2.	12	10	13	14	7	10	12
3.	13	13	11	15	17	14	18
4.	13	15	15	18	18	18	13
5.	16	17	17	18	18	13	18

© RBP Books   www.summerbridgeactivities.com   Math Connection—Grade 3—RBP3799

Answer Pages

Page 29

1.	4	6	7	7	3	9
2.	3	4	4	4	3	8
3.	6	8	5	9	2	6
4.	3	5	3	9	3	6
5.	5	8	7	5	9	7
6.	9	4	7	8	3	2

Page 30

1.	8	6	8	7	7	4
2.	9	8	2	2	4	9
3.	7	3	4	5	5	3
4.	5	2	8	2	8	9
5.	9	2	2	9	7	7
6.	9	5	8	3	8	6

Page 31

1.	5	7	5	2	8	11
2.	15	7	11	14	5	14
3.	4	13	9	3	10	13
4.	6	6	8	9	12	8
5.	15	9	17	3	3	18
6.	4	8	5	8	16	10

Page 32

1.	12	11	7	4	15	9
2.	15	6	7	12	14	9
3.	7	11	11	6	3	4
4.	3	13	3	13	5	15
5.	6	5	3	12	11	5
6.	17	8	4	14	5	16

Page 33

1.	7	4	7	3
2.	15	9	15	6
3.	13	8	13	5
4.	11	4	11	7
5.	14	8	14	6
6.	12	7	12	5

7. $5 + 9 = 14$ $9 + 5 = 14$ $14 - 9 = 5$ $14 - 5 = 9$
8. $8 + 9 = 17$ $9 + 8 = 17$ $17 - 8 = 9$ $17 - 9 = 8$
9. $6 + 7 = 13$ $7 + 6 = 13$ $13 - 6 = 7$ $13 - 7 = 6$
10. $7 + 8 = 15$ $8 + 7 = 15$ $15 - 7 = 8$ $15 - 8 = 7$

Page 34

1. $13 - 2 = 11$ cans   **2.** $7 + 5 = 12$ cards
3. $7 + 3 + 4 = 14$ runs   **4.** $11 - 3 = 8$ glasses
5. $12 - 4 = 8$ balloons   **6.** $3 + 8 = 11$ cards

Page 35

1. $9 - 4 = 5$ 5 pots
2. $17 - 11 = 6$ 6 boxes
3. $15 - 8 = 7$ 7 more cards
4. $7 + 4 = 11$ 11 fish
5. $16 - 7 = 9$ 9 pieces of candy
6. $5 + 8 = 13$ 13 books

Page 36

1.	12	9	12	10	12	9
2.	13	13	12	10	11	18
3.	9	8	8	7	9	6
4.	6	7	8	4	8	9

5. $7 - 5 = 2$ kittens are left
6. $9 + 8 = 17$ pages

Page 37

1.	11	13	13	13	13	10
2.	12	12	13	10	14	17
3.	8	7	7	8	8	5
4.	5	8	7	3	9	7

5. $7 + 8 = 15$ 15 cousins
6. $13 - 8 = 5$ 5 cousins are girls

Page 38

1.	65	89	78	58	85	69
2.	99	93	97	99	59	89
3.	89	96	78	79	59	59
4.	87	99	96	89	87	71
5.	88	85	67	78	79	86
6.	86	79	49	99	85	74

Page 39

1.	49	59	98	89	96	49
2.	73	87	27	68	95	57
3.	86	75	67	59	98	96
4.	86	69	77	74	94	78
5.	48	59	98	79	69	99
6.	66	97	56	66	66	78

Page 40

1.	54	40	22	65	61	15
2.	26	20	24	23	51	50
3.	32	23	4	60	24	24
4.	22	10	40	15	26	16
5.	72	41	50	34	41	63
6.	37	62	41	42	33	42

Page 41

1.	82	61	56	22	21	25
2.	57	21	22	46	31	24
3.	51	72	61	41	40	57
4.	12	31	11	82	31	45
5.	22	22	43	16	34	52
6.	42	20	22	13	54	22

Page 42

1.	51	92	81	86	64	90
2.	94	130	92	92	103	75
3.	92	111	70	114	130	140
4.	81	83	83	61	46	86
5.	70	62	96	90	81	76
6.	74	80	75	151	94	65

Answer Pages

Page 43

1.	94	64	76	71	80	65
2.	74	97	90	76	65	80
3.	91	72	61	74	90	92
4.	73	85	73	60	101	91
5.	102	93	80	85	81	90
6.	76	72	91	101	91	120

Page 44

1.	19	79	19	26	16	49
2.	19	58	14	59	28	32
3.	28	68	36	39	14	47
4.	25	39	59	38	48	24
5.	38	29	49	8	58	19
6.	69	18	47	28	36	28

Page 45

1.	5	14	36	28	47	54
2.	19	35	43	29	14	22
3.	43	26	18	19	19	47
4.	23	24	17	42	43	26
5.	39	17	38	19	28	35
6.	12	38	26	37	42	56

Page 46

1.	58	66	28	71	92
2.	24	59	19	81	32
3.	60	142	12	57	92
4.	33	85	18	87	61
5.	39	47	19	92	89
6.	113	74	19	82	16

Page 47

1.	130	49	16	83	76
2.	35	70	101	17	38
3.	33	28	119	29	95
4.	102	91	53	62	18
5.	16	77	42	19	110
6.	16	55	83	33	55

Page 48

1. $42 - 28 = 14$ Sam's team scored 14 more points.
2. $57 + 26 = 83$ Jan has 83 shells.
3. $82 - 15 = 67$ Nathan gave 67 cars to his cousins.
4. $43 + 38 = 81$ The bike shop has 81 bikes.
5. $35 - 28 = 7$ Alexis sold 7 more boxes.
6. $34 - 8 = 26$ Phil has 26 books left.

Page 49

1. $25 + 38 = 63$ 63 golf balls
2. $82 - 76 = 6$ 6 more cans
3. $75 - 56 = 19$ 19 more books
4. $68 + 17 = 85$ 85 rocks
5. $74 - 25 = 49$ 49 pieces of gum
6. $37 - 28 = 9$ 9 dolls

Page 50

1.	76	77	89	99	88	65
2.	34	42	42	12	43	61
3.	91	123	75	112	131	95
4.	44	42	36	43	16	12

5. $50 - 37 = 13$ 13 more miles
6. $27 + 34 = 61$ 61 miles

Page 51

1.	58	79	89	94	68	75
2.	45	56	33	45	56	51
3.	91	144	110	112	61	75
4.	55	39	38	34	67	47

5. $82 - 69 = 13$ 13 more books
6. $47 + 58 = 105$ 105 pages

Page 52

1.	885	778	988	998	527
2.	594	986	969	789	919
3.	788	985	867	877	798
4.	786	786	879	769	888
5.	985	678	899	957	898
6.	956	699	969	889	859

Page 53

1.	431	213	225	236	223
2.	553	322	812	121	205
3.	63	137	462	414	142
4.	633	342	704	312	148
5.	220	414	260	316	541

Page 54

1.	940	610	1,091	1,311	420
2.	611	613	617	1,211	1,062
3.	791	763	793	591	366
4.	970	662	696	990	781
5.	749	809	759	919	946
6.	927	635	748	920	810

Page 55

1.	451	702	816	1,192	830
2.	823	851	1,044	1,013	605
3.	900	813	1,011	1,177	1,021
4.	613	821	862	750	929
5.	1,180	1,405	872	894	831
6.	1,174	974	611	794	890

Page 56

1.	433	872	797	622	810
2.	825	847	944	771	625
3.	910	510	794	755	879
4.	808	927	786	728	781
5.	1,061	1,135	1,072	809	619
6.	903	1,552	604	1,134	970

© RBP Books   www.summerbridgeactivities.com   Math Connection—Grade 3—RBP3799

Page 57

1.	699	269	469	429	257
2.	187	292	739	289	228
3.	424	338	429	449	608
4.	584	193	691	84	470
5.	281	427	528	391	206

Page 58

1.	224	299	287	228	455
2.	383	269	578	270	349
3.	335	147	141	443	212
4.	465	229	475	188	411
5.	434	469	558	569	273
6.	591	397	182	359	112

Page 59

1.	606	179	324	198	412
2.	165	369	525	235	347
3.	427	439	251	466	152
4.	289	488	196	387	424
5.	437	553	588	326	316
6.	436	387	688	268	382

Page 60

1.	1,025	307	1,226	1,012	462
2.	732	921	118	1,119	349
3.	198	822	438	1,381	463
4.	823	652	507	920	508
5.	426	459	1,082	1,024	865
6.	1,234	394	831	904	928

Page 61

1.	610	2.	294	3.	574	4.	719
5.	489	6.	641				

Page 62

1. 346 − 188 = 158   Roberto has 158 cards left.
2. 121 + 699 = 820   The school has 820 labels.
3. 623 + 17 = 640   Alex has 640 rocks.
4. 435 − 178 = 257   The pet store has 257 fish left.
5. 728 − 649 = 79   Devin has 79 more coins than Kate.
6. 321 + 399 = 720   They have 720 marbles altogether.

Page 63

1. 348 − 239 = 109   109 pennies
2. 479 + 742 = 1,221   1,221 cans
3. 371 − 138 = 233   233 televisions
4. 202 − 189 = 13   13 pounds less
5. 879 + 932 = 1,811   1,811 books
6. 487 − 399 = 88   88 more points

Page 64

1.	943	495	769	683	898
2.	554	322	634	513	326
3.	1,131	667	1,500	1,221	936
4.	354	694	486	278	357
5.	661 − 478 = 183		183 more points		
6.	322 + 489 = 811		811 bottle caps		

Page 65

1.	955	946	896	849	689
2.	322	432	422	331	243
3.	1,120	823	1,011	1,104	984
4.	493	428	253	287	425
5.	489 + 492 = 981		981 third graders		
6.	987 − 899 = 88		88 more kindergartners		

Page 66

1.	8,500	6,712	9,809	9,080	4,401
2.	6,308	13,046	8,180	11,055	9,742
3.	8,066	11,195	10,191	9,809	11,207
4.	11,906	7,600	7,424	11,039	10,889
5.	5,008	10,087	6,041	11,817	11,817
6.	12,570	7,715	5,026	6,102	12,079

Page 67

1.	4,406	1,296	2,067	2,947	2,087
2.	4,728	6,035	3,760	5,965	1,082
3.	3,559	5,032	4,802	2,058	2,758
4.	909	4,063	1,879	6,077	7,367
5.	3,696	4,086	1,274	4,663	4,977

Page 68

1.	10,107	1,401	4,145	6,230
2.	3,545	3,615	2,876	5,383
3.	7,123	2,521	8,807	6,721
4.	4,362	8,295	5,902	2,891
5.	8,669	5,225	4,703	7,993

Page 69

1a. 2,479 + 3,210 = 5,689
5,689 people went to the concert.
1b. 3,210 − 2,479 = 731
731 more people attended on Saturday night than Friday night.
2a. 1,324 + 1,129 = 2,453
2,453 graduated from the two high schools.
2b. 1,324 − 1,129 = 195
195 more students graduated from East High.
3a. 8,721 − 7,820 = 901
901 more people live in Littletown.
3b. 8,721 + 7,820 = 16,541
16,541 people live in the two towns.

Page 70

1.	6 feet	2.	9 inches	3.	1 inch
4.	20 inches	5.	2 inches	6.	1 inch
7.	2 + 2 + 1 + 1 = 6 inches				

Page 71

1.	9 cm	2.	8 cm	3.	5 cm
4.	5 cm	5.	7 cm	6.	7 cm

Page 72

1.	>	2.	>	3.	=
4.	<	5.	>		
6.	32 inches	7.	3 inches		

Answer Pages

Page 73
1.	5:00	2.	6:30	3.	3:20
4.	10:10	5.	1:40	6.	6:50
7.	6:00	8.	12:30	9.	3:55

Page 74

1. 2. 3. 4. 5.

6. 7. 8. 9.

Page 75
1.	12:19	2.	6:17	3.	8:33	4.	11:19

5. 6. 7. 8.

Page 76
1.	7:55	2.	4:40	3.	3:24
4.	5:43	5.	8:21	6.	11 hours

Page 77
1.	37 minutes	2.	9:00 p.m.
3.	7 minutes	4.	8:47 p.m.
5.	1 hour 21 minutes	6.	3 hours

Page 78
1. 25, 50, 60, 70, 71, 72, 73, 74 total 74¢
2. 25, 50, 60, 70, 75, 80, 81, 82 total 82¢
3. 50, 60, 65, 70, 75, 76, 77, 78 total 78¢
4. 50, 60, 70, 80, 85, 90, 91, 92 total 92¢
5. 25, 50, 60, 65, 70, 75, 76, 77 total 77¢
6. 50, 75, 80, 85, 86, 87, 88, 89 total 89¢

Page 79
1.	68¢	2.	93¢	3.	92¢
4.	94¢	5.	90¢	6.	92¢

Page 80
1.	$1.55	2.	$2.48	3.	$7.45
4.	$10.85	5.	$17.17	6.	$69.00

Page 81
1.	$2.55	2.	$7.40	3.	$16.06
4.	$4.01	5.	$2.84	6.	$13.01

Page 82
1.	65¢	2.	79¢	3.	$1.10
4.	$3.62	5.	$10.78	6.	$40.78
7.	$13.70	8.	$21.75	9.	$1.60
10.	$1.76	11.	$8.50	12.	$20.95
13.	$10.90	14.	$62.10	15.	$31.80
16.	$19.85				

Page 83
1. $17.22 + 5.00 = $22.22 Gina had $22.22.
2. $18.77 − 14.50 = $4.27 Matt would have $4.27 left.
3. $3.50 + 4.00 + 10.00 = $17.50 Jon got $17.50.
4. $87.00 − 53.00 = $34.00 Len needs $34.00 more.
5. $20.00 + 12.00 = $32.00 Dan has $32.00.
6. $18.00 − 6.00 = $12.00 Emma needs $12.00 more.

Page 84
1.	$12.28	2.	$36.50	3.	$9.51
4.	$96.26	5.	$47.00	6.	$12.74

Page 85
1.	2 cm	2.	8 cm	3.	6:45	4.	3:27
5.	10:32	6.	$1.23	7.	$11.46	8.	$2.15

Page 86
1.	1 in	2.	2 in	3.	6 in
4.	7:15	5.	4:47	6.	8:12
7.	$1.86	8.	$7.90	9.	8:46

Page 87
1. Wednesday night television shows
2. 8:30
3. Channel 5
4. *Eating Right*
5. 2 hours
6. 4 channels
7. 5 shows
8. Answers may vary.

Page 88
1. 5
2. $\frac{2}{4}, \frac{3}{6}, \frac{4}{8}$
3. $\frac{2}{6}$
4. $\frac{3}{6}$
5. $\frac{3}{4}$
6. $\frac{6}{8}$
7. $\frac{2}{6}$
8. $\frac{1}{1}, \frac{2}{2}, \frac{3}{3}, \frac{4}{4}, \frac{5}{5}, \frac{6}{6}, \frac{7}{7}, \frac{8}{8}$

Page 89

www.summerbridgeactivities.com **Math Connection—Grade 3—RBP3799**

Page 90

x	1	2	3	4	5	6	7	8	9
1	1	2	3	4	5	6	7	8	9
2	2	4	6	8	10	12	14	16	18
3	3	6	9	12	15	18	21	24	27
4	4	8	12	16	20	24	28	32	36
5	5	10	15	20	25	30	35	40	45
6	6	12	18	24	30	36	42	48	54
7	7	14	21	28	35	42	49	56	63
8	8	16	24	32	40	48	56	64	72
9	9	18	27	36	45	54	63	72	81

1. the number itself
2. skip counting by 2s
3. skip counting by 5s
4. 9
5. 12

Page 91

1. 9   6   12   21   5
2. 8   9   27   18   4
3. 12   10   4   2   0
4. 16   3   14   24   15
5. 2   7   6   0   6
6. 8   0   1   18   0

Page 92

1. 25   48   24   35   36
2. 8   18   20   12   42
3. 12   6   10   0   4
4. 0   30   54   16   15
5. 45   24   40   0   5
6. 20   28   32   30   36

Page 93

1. 56   21   36   64   7
2. 63   40   42   0   16
3. 35   24   45   81   14
4. 9   32   49   63   54
5. 0   28   72   18   8
6. 27   48   56   72   0

Page 94

1. 4   6   15   6   12
2. 16   10   12   8   2
3. 14   18   18   16   20
4. 27   30   24   21   24
5. 16   30   40   63   64
6. 20   72   42   35   32
7. 36   28   56   81   36
8. 20   25   45   48   28

Page 95

1. 54   30   18   36   42   24   12   48
2. 72   40   24   48   56   32   16   64
3. 27   15   9   18   21   12   6   24
4. 63   35   21   42   49   28   14   56
5. 45   25   15   30   35   20   10   40
6. 81   45   27   54   63   36   18   72
7. 36   20   12   24   28   16   8   32
8. 9   5   3   6   7   4   2   8
9. 18   10   6   12   14   8   4   16

Page 96

1. 18   30   48   54   24   42
2. 48   64   40   72   56   32
3. 24   36   16   20   32   12
4. 15   20   35   30   45   25
5. 45   72   27   54   81   63
6. 42   35   63   28   49   56

Page 97

1. 6 x 9 = 54 – Randy has 54 marbles.
2. 4 x 8 = 32 – Stan has 32 cards.
3. 5 x 9 = 45 – Jennifer jumped 45 times.
4. 6 x 5 = 30 – Zach runs 30 miles each week.
5. 7 x 4 = 28 – There were 28 skaters.
6. 8 x 6 = 48 – They had 48 bandages.

Page 98

1. 9 x 9 = 81   81 boxes of cereal
2. 8 x 7 = 56   56 students
3. 7 x 6 = 42   42 pictures
4. 8 x 9 = 72   72 baseball cards
5. 2 x 7 = 14   14 pages
6. 5 x 8 = 40   40 marbles

Page 99

1. 3   2. 4   3. 3
4. 4   5. 2   6. 6

Page 100

1. 21 ÷ 3 = 7   2. 30 ÷ 5 = 6
3. 36 ÷ 9 = 4   4. 18 ÷ 6 = 3

Page 101

1. 1   2   3   4   5   6   7   8   9   10
2. 1   3   5   7   9   2   4   6   8   10
3. 1   2   4   6   8   10   3   5   7   9
4. 1   3   6   9   8   5   2   7   10   4
5. 1   2   9   3   8   4   10   7   6   5
6. 1   2   4   6   10   8   3   5   7   9

Math Connection—Grade 3—RBP3799   www.summerbridgeactivities.com   © RBP Books

Page 102
1. 3, 2
2. 4, 3
3. 3, 5
4. 2, 5
5. 8, 2
6. 5, 4
7. 4, 6
8. 7, 4
9. 4, 9
10. 2, 8
11. 8, 6
12. 6, 9
13. 8, 7, 9, 8
14. 7, 7, 4, 5
15. 9, 8, 8, 4
16. 6, 9, 7, 6

Page 103
1. 6   6   7   9
2. 7   7   9   9
3. 7   9   9   7
4. 6   4   8   6
5. 4   7   5   8
6. 4   6   5   6
7. 7   8   4   8
8. 8   3   9   9

Page 104
1. $12 \div 2 = 6$ There will be 6 goldfish in each tank.
2. $8 \div 2 = 4$ Deb will wear 4 bracelets on each wrist.
3. $16 \div 4 = 4$ The team scored 4 points each quarter.
4. $15 \div 3 = 5$ Nick has 5 trophies on each shelf.
5. $18 \div 6 = 3$ Jan sewed 3 buttons on each pocket.
6. $35 \div 7 = 5$ Kelly will need 5 pages.

Page 105
1. $72 \div 8 = 9$ stamps on each page
2. $56 \div 7 = 8$ rocks in each group
3. $81 \div 9 = 9$ necklaces
4. $21 \div 7 = 3$ miles every day
5. $42 \div 6 = 7$ rabbits in each cage
6. $45 \div 5 = 9$ minutes each day

Page 106
1. $5 \times 9 = 45$ $9 \times 5 = 45$ $45 \div 5 = 9$ $45 \div 9 = 5$
2. $5 \times 6 = 30$ $6 \times 5 = 30$ $30 \div 5 = 6$ $30 \div 6 = 5$
3. $4 \times 3 = 12$ $3 \times 4 = 12$ $12 \div 3 = 4$ $12 \div 4 = 3$
4. $2 \times 7 = 14$ $7 \times 2 = 14$ $14 \div 7 = 2$ $14 \div 2 = 7$
5. $3 \times 8 = 24$ $8 \times 3 = 24$ $24 \div 3 = 8$ $24 \div 8 = 3$
6. $2 \times 9 = 18$ $9 \times 2 = 18$ $18 \div 9 = 2$ $18 \div 2 = 9$
7. $9 \times 3 = 27$ $3 \times 9 = 27$ $27 \div 9 = 3$ $27 \div 3 = 9$
8. $2 \times 8 = 16$ $8 \times 2 = 16$ $16 \div 8 = 2$ $16 \div 2 = 8$
9. $4 \times 7 = 28$ $7 \times 4 = 28$ $28 \div 7 = 4$ $28 \div 4 = 7$
10. $4 \times 9 = 36$ $9 \times 4 = 36$ $36 \div 9 = 4$ $36 \div 4 = 9$
11. $2 \times 6 = 12$ $6 \times 2 = 12$ $12 \div 6 = 2$ $12 \div 2 = 6$
12. $4 \times 8 = 32$ $8 \times 4 = 32$ $32 \div 8 = 4$ $32 \div 4 = 8$

Page 107
1. $7 \times 8 = 56$ $8 \times 7 = 56$ $56 \div 7 = 8$ $56 \div 8 = 7$
   $6 \times 7 = 42$ $7 \times 6 = 42$ $42 \div 6 = 7$ $42 \div 7 = 6$
   $4 \times 5 = 20$ $5 \times 4 = 20$ $20 \div 4 = 5$ $20 \div 5 = 4$
2. $9 \times 8 = 72$ $8 \times 9 = 72$ $72 \div 8 = 9$ $72 \div 9 = 8$
   $9 \times 7 = 63$ $7 \times 9 = 63$ $63 \div 9 = 7$ $63 \div 7 = 9$
   $9 \times 6 = 54$ $6 \times 9 = 54$ $54 \div 9 = 6$ $54 \div 6 = 9$
3. $7 \times 7 = 49$ $49 \div 7 = 7$
   $8 \times 8 = 64$ $64 \div 8 = 8$
   $9 \times 9 = 81$ $81 \div 9 = 9$
4. $8 \times 6 = 48$ $6 \times 8 = 48$ $48 \div 6 = 8$ $48 \div 8 = 6$
   $4 \times 8 = 32$ $8 \times 4 = 32$ $32 \div 4 = 8$ $32 \div 8 = 4$
   $9 \times 4 = 36$ $4 \times 9 = 36$ $36 \div 9 = 4$ $36 \div 4 = 9$

Page 108
1. 48   21   16   36   14
2. 36   24   16   12   15
3. 64   30   6   28   18
4. 30   56   20   49   72
5. 9   5   8   8
6. 9   6   7   7
7. 8   6   3   7
8. 5   9   8   4

Page 109
1. 40   28   24   63   42
2. 32   56   25   24   9
3. 72   40   16   42   12
4. 35   48   63   36   72
5. 2   6   7   7
6. 5   3   4   6
7. 9   7   7   3
8. 6   2   7   7

Page 110
1. 240   330   770   90   30
2. 40   440   70   420   720
3. 280   860   510   290   820
4. 80   230   660   830   130
5. 170   350   420   180   990
6. 60   700   890   410   200

Page 111
1. 48   22   26   39
2. 33   28   36   44
3. 13   66   66   64
4. 84   48   44   63
5. 99   96   93   62

  www.summerbridgeactivities.com   Math Connection—Grade 3—RBP3799

Answer Pages

Page 112
1.	70	77	14	80
2.	88	46	36	84
3.	23	88	66	65
4.	88	80	42	99
5.	55	15	66	60
6.	80	82	78	96

Page 113
1.	90	70	91	72	110
2.	84	100	192	161	112
3.	78	312	220	204	117
4.	252	270	288	112	56
5.	210	126	154	170	141
6.	38	198	336	252	415

Page 114
1.	78	162	176	174	195	198
2.	240	168	648	175	144	301
3.	96	216	132	387	222	174
4.	156	116	256	98	315	584
5.	290	108	108	372	111	477
6.	335	184	65	315	264	378
7.	504	234	232	306	110	372

Page 115
1.	150	144	368	448	340	378	224
2.	90	344	270	162	126	512	165
3.	324	145	328	264	365	81	136
4.	308	340	376	518	348	200	64
5.	135	192	462	485	330	144	312
6.	238	54	558	260	152	276	160
7.	294	504	567	352	392	130	120

Page 116
1.	354	90	434	405	552	207	196
2.	330	272	378	455	658	424	232
3.	483	112	432	456	258	297	616
4.	294	558	72	132	203	252	265
5.	185	288	380	260	168	462	738
6.	264	333	182	153	192	154	324

Page 117
1.	441	195	345	576	469	496	272
2.	385	639	420	600	304	553	666
3.	574	510	267	747	440	602	640
4.	630	828	768	570	396	470	588
5.	119	133	161	322	259	413	441
6.	504	168	736	664	376	608	464
7.	756	243	810	513	675	594	342

Page 118
1.	48	75	136	240	364	60	135
2.	108	135	228	45	189	195	322
3.	440	78	184	132	240	177	55
4.	112	222	378	477	98	100	70
5.	352	348	64	87	288	329	285
6.	72	156	266	196	392	280	288

Page 119
1.	29 x 3 = 87	87 cookies
2.	12 x 7 = 84	84 inches
3.	17 x 6 = 102	102 miles
4.	48 x 7 = 336	336 pages
5.	50 x 5 = 250	250 trading cards
6.	73 x 4 = 292	292 stamps

Page 120
1.	260	750	830	370	540
2.	66	84	68	28	66
3.	188	265	434	729	222
4.	432	693	336	272	435
5.	75 x 4 = 300	300 meters			
6.	37 x 3 = 111	111 yards			

Page 121
1.	460	630	490	920	380
2.	93	82	86	39	60
3.	528	657	156	135	330
4.	518	664	438	116	204
5.	120 hours				
6.	24 miles				

Page 122
1.	4	2
2.	7	1
3.	2	2
4.	6	1
5.	2	1
6.	3	3

Page 123
1.	7r1	5r2	4r3	3r4
2.	6r1	3r3	3r2	5r3
3.	7r7	9r1	5r1	4r4
4.	4r2	2r1	3r1	6r2
5.	4r1	3r4	4r6	4r6
6.	3r4	2r4	2r1	5r2

Page 124
1.	14	13r2	12r2	21r1
2.	12	11r4	15	15r2
3.	19	21	18r2	16r1
4.	14r1	11r6	11r1	11r3
5.	25r1	14r3	14r2	16

 © RBP Books

Answer Pages

Page 125
1. 3   3   3   4   4
2. 8   7   7   8   7
3. 6r1   3r3   3r3   3r1   3r2
4. 6r1   5r4   3r1   5r2   8r2
5. 11   13   13   11   12
6. 13r1   12r1   12r1   17r1   19r3

Page 126
1. 3r5   4r6   8r3   8r4   7r7
2. 3r3   3r5   7r2   7r5   9r2
3. 4r5   9r1   5r2   9r2   8r4
4. 19   17r1   18r2   14r1   15r2
5. 12r2   28   26   22   22r1
6. 13r1   13r2   29r2   19r1   24r1

Page 127
1. 7   8   6   7   9
2. 22   41   19   23   16
3. 19r1   11r3   16r3   13r3   21r2
4. 15r3   29r1   10r2   14r3   27r2
5. $47 \div 6 = 7r5$ 7 biscuits with 5 left over
6. $25 \div 5 = 5$ 5 miles

Page 128
1. 9   7   4   8   5
2. 21   23   17   13   12
3. 15r2   14r3   14r2   14r1   32r1
4. 17r3   32r2   13r1   19r3   24r1
5. $12 \div 6 = 2$ 2 hours each day
6. $96 \div 8 = 12$ 12 chickens in each coop

Page 129
1. square, rectangle, trapezoid, rhombus
2. square
3. triangle
4. circle
5. pentagon
6. hexagon
7. octagon
8. square, rectangle, hexagon, rhombus, octagon
9. a rhombus has 2 sets of parallel lines, a trapezoid has one set

Page 130
Answers will vary.

Page 131
1. yes   **2.** no   **3.** no
4. yes   **5.** yes   **6.** yes
7–9. Answers may vary.

Page 132
1. 6   **2.** 2, 3
3. 2, 4   **4.** 4, 2

Page 133
1. $\frac{1}{6}$ **2.** $\frac{3}{8}$ **3.** $\frac{3}{4}$
4. $\frac{5}{8}$ **5.** $\frac{11}{32}$ **6.** $\frac{7}{12}$

Page 134
1. $\frac{2}{6} = \frac{1}{3}$ **2.** $\frac{3}{4} > \frac{1}{2}$ **3.** $\frac{3}{4} = \frac{6}{8}$
4. $\frac{2}{4} > \frac{2}{8}$ **5.** $\frac{1}{2} < \frac{3}{4}$ **6.** $\frac{1}{8} < \frac{1}{4}$

Page 135
1. $\frac{2}{6}$ $\frac{3}{9}$ $\frac{4}{12}$ $\frac{5}{15}$
2. $\frac{2}{8}$ $\frac{3}{12}$ $\frac{4}{16}$ $\frac{5}{20}$
3. $\frac{4}{6}$ $\frac{6}{9}$ $\frac{8}{12}$ $\frac{10}{15}$
4. $\frac{6}{8}$ $\frac{9}{12}$ $\frac{12}{16}$ $\frac{15}{20}$
5. $\frac{8}{10}$ $\frac{9}{21}$ $\frac{16}{28}$ $\frac{21}{28}$
6. $\frac{14}{16}$ $\frac{15}{18}$ $\frac{12}{42}$ $\frac{8}{20}$

Page 136
1. $\frac{1}{2}$ $\frac{1}{3}$ $\frac{1}{3}$
2. $\frac{2}{3}$ $\frac{1}{6}$ $\frac{1}{3}$
3. $\frac{1}{4}$ $\frac{1}{4}$ $\frac{1}{5}$
4. $\frac{1}{7}$ $\frac{1}{5}$ $\frac{1}{3}$

Page 137
1. $4\frac{2}{3}$ $2\frac{2}{5}$ $4\frac{1}{4}$ $6\frac{1}{2}$
2. $1\frac{5}{7}$ $3\frac{3}{5}$ $6\frac{3}{4}$ $4\frac{3}{5}$
3. $3\frac{2}{3}$ $3\frac{3}{4}$ $4\frac{4}{5}$ $6\frac{1}{3}$
4. $9\frac{1}{2}$ $8\frac{1}{4}$ $7\frac{1}{3}$ $9\frac{1}{3}$
5. $2\frac{1}{4}$ $4\frac{1}{3}$ $6\frac{1}{2}$ $5\frac{1}{4}$

Page 138
1. $\frac{4}{8} < \frac{5}{6}$
2. $\frac{4}{16} = \frac{1}{4}$
3. $\frac{4}{8}$
4. $\frac{3}{6}$
5. $\frac{1}{3}$ $\frac{1}{2}$ $\frac{1}{3}$ $\frac{1}{3}$
6. $5\frac{2}{3}$ $2\frac{3}{5}$ $5\frac{1}{2}$ $4\frac{2}{3}$

© RBP Books   www.summerbridgeactivities.com   Math Connection—Grade 3—RBP3799

Answer Pages

Page 139

1. $\frac{4}{6} = \frac{2}{3}$
2. $\frac{4}{10} < \frac{4}{5}$
3. $\frac{2}{6}$
4. $\frac{8}{16}$
5. $\frac{1}{2}$ $\frac{1}{3}$ $\frac{2}{3}$ $\frac{3}{4}$
6. $3\frac{2}{5}$ $2\frac{1}{6}$ $6\frac{1}{3}$ $3\frac{1}{4}$

Page 140

1. equal
2. yellow
3. zero
4. 2
5. 4

Page 141

1. December
2. July, August, September
3. October
4. January
5. January
6. September
7. Unlikely
8. Yes

Page 142

1. diagonal lines
2. every other one going down the columns
3. skipping two going down the columns, skipping every other column
4. one diagonal line

Page 143

1.

2	5
3	7
4	9
5	11
6	13
7	15
8	17

2.

2	4
3	7
4	10
5	13
6	16
7	19
8	22

3.

2	11
3	16
4	21
5	26
6	31
7	36
8	41

4.

2	0
3	4
4	8
5	12
6	16
7	20
8	24

5. [ ] x 3 + 2
6. [ ] – 2 x 3

Page 144

1. 12   7   4   8
2. 3   8   13   17
3. 2   4   8   3
4. 8   12   16   4

Page 145

1. 13   17   12   12   12   11   13
2. 39   76   65   86   85   88   95
3. 9   13   18   13   13   16   13
4. 120   118   133   119   84   104   123
5. 166   1,008   626   851   1,223   910   1,105
6. 14,020   11,236   8,381   9,930   10,701   12,351

Page 146

1. 6   5   3   2   4   3   3
2. 41   51   22   52   25   33   42
3. 66   29   26   31   35   45   40
4. 680   507   582   283   596   307   225
5. 477   280   199   289   618   518   359
6. 4,032   2,110   5,221   8,200   2,214   4,234

Page 147

1. 14   15   27   20   12   35   24
2. 10   28   54   56   40   45   56
3. 72   63   64   81   42   72   45
4. 90   350   120   80   540   320   490
5. 132   148   87   90   744   406   192
6. 91   344   328   84   558   783   340

Page 148

1. 2   6   8   7
2. 1   5   9   7
3. 5   7   8   6
4. 8   9   8   7
5. 9   8   7   3   4   9
6. 9   2   7   6   6   3
7. 6r2   8r2   6r4   7r2   8r3   4r4
8. 7 x 8 = 56   8 x 7 = 56   56 ÷ 7 = 8   56 ÷ 8 = 7
9. 6 x 7 = 42   7 x 6 = 42   42 ÷ 6 = 7   42 ÷ 7 = 6

Page 149

1. 20   24   63   21   30   16   72
2. 9   4   7   8   8   6
3. 9   35   7   16
4. 42   4   6   49
5. 24   3   4   54
6. 60   9   64   6
7. 604   829   1,047   513   1,007   508
8. 16   54   106   83   879   450